God, Guns & Greed

A Dangerous Path for America

by Leah L. Burton

God, Guns & Greed by Leah L. Burton
Published 2011 by Lexovien, LLC
http://www.lexovien.com
FaceBook: Lexovien
Twitter: Lexopub

2711 Centerville Road
Suite 120 #7385
Wilmington, DE 19808

Lexovien edition published September 1, 2011
Print Book ISBN-13 : 9781937638023
Print Book ISBN-10: 1937638022

Preface

A dangerous game of God, Guns & Greed is afoot in America as the common interests of these three sectors align and cross-pollinate.

While their motivations differ, all lead to a similar attack on secular America. While some of them seek to institutionalize religion under the authority of the Dominionists, others are driven by economic and sovereignty platforms.

Their end goal is the same:
to privatize government.

Grasping the true seriousness of this understandably challenges the rational minds of most Americans who have always thought there is a separation between Church and State.

No more.

For America it is no longer simply a fight of Republican vs. Democrat.

It is now

Theocracy vs. Freedom.

iv

Dedication

Dedicated to my supportive and loving spouse whose belief in me has never wavered; to my daughter and her daughter - that they never know the realities of living in a theocracy; to those who have encouraged me and supported my work as I have reinvented how to convey this message even in the face of aggressive push back and opposition.

To Alex Bird for her wealth of knowledge on Dominionism and research that confirmed so much of what I had experienced and learned about this extremism in my life. Elizabeth Sholes for the Chapter on *Imbedded Inequality*, and "Sarah Jones" from PoliticusUSA.com for her Chapter, *Igniting & Exciting Fear*.

And to my politically secular republican father, a well known Alaskan Commissioner and life-long State Trooper, for his support in every way - even when up against uncomfortable criticism in no uncertain terms from his former cohorts in Alaska's Republican community. Priceless!

I also want to thank Dr. Anthea Butler for writing the Foreword for this book validating this discussion from a professional academic voice and researcher of Dominionism.

And to Lexovien Publishing, LLC for having the foresight and courage to make this book happen when other publishers were too afraid of touching such a controversial project. We all owe them a tremendous debt of gratitude!

And to *all* Americans – liberal or conservative – who hold that our freedoms are worth fighting for.

Foreword

I am pleased to write the introduction for Leah Burton's book *God, Guns and Greed: A Dangerous Path for America*." Leah's long-term work researching and writing about Political Dominionism holds an important message for the future of our nation, and more immediately, the upcoming 2012 election. Burton's book is a warning about the marriage of the political and religious words that seek to destroy our constitutional rights, and turn America into a nation based on their narrow interpretations of biblical law.

I have firsthand experience watching the rise of Political Dominionism as a seminary student at Fuller Seminary in Pasadena, California. My coursework there coincided with one of the leaders in the movement, C. Peter Wagner, preparing to retire and take his teachings about "spiritual mapping" to the next level of religious entrepreneurship. The New Apostolic Reformation (NAR), a term coined by Wagner, and their support of many of the Republican candidates for the 2012 Presidential race is a new recasting of the Religious Right with a much more dangerous agenda. Rather than simply preparing for the rapture and the return of Christ, they are ready to "occupy" until Jesus returns, comes, and more importantly, take their place on one of the "seven mountains of power." If all of this sounds farfetched, by the time you read *Guns, God, and Greed* cover to cover, you will be convinced.

What *God, Guns, and Greed* shows is the rapid rise of this movement, and the manner in which religious organizations, politicians, and religious figures have linked together to form an alliance that threatens the "wall of separation" between Church and State.

Burton's book is important and timely work, for it shows the connections and depths to which the movement has taken over the political scene. One major example of how the movement has escalated is Governor Rick Perry's prayer meeting "The Response," in Houston, Texas. The meeting drew over 30,000 people for a day of prayer and fasting for America, while being exhorted by NAR leadership. The prayer meeting's sign up list is currently being used as a voting and recruiting tool for the American Family association. So much for the separation of church and state that Jefferson hoped for.

Read *God, Guns, and Greed*, and I promise that you will never look at right wing conservative religion the same way again. Share the book with others you know. Now is a crucial time in the life of our nation to reaffirm the words of Thomas Jefferson who said, "I contemplate with solemn reverence the act of the whole American People which declared that their legislature should 'make no law respecting an establishment of religion, or prohibiting the free exercise thereof,' thus building a wall of separation between church and state."

God, Guns, and Greed is a step in the right direction to get the national conversation about the role of religion in politics back on track.

Anthea D. Butler
Associate Professor of Religious Studies
University of Pennsylvania

Table of Contents

1 What the...?! A Nation Collectively Gasps!

"She's not — she's not from these parts and she's not from Washington. But when you get to know her, you're going to be as impressed as I am." - *2008 Presidential candidate U.S. Senator John McCain*

It was August 29th, 2008 and I was weeks into writing a humorous non-fiction book that made me burst out laughing as I worked peacefully in the privacy of my home office. I was on Chapter 12 and flying along with ease, enjoying my life as it had evolved. My daughter was grown and in college and my family was moving in a very pleasant direction, settling into a rhythm that was still new to me even though I was several years post-political ... or so I thought.

My sense of calm and balance was disrupted in a matter of minutes as I heard a breaking news announcement interrupt my radio listening pleasure - Sarah Louise Heath Palin had just been announced as the Vice Presidential nominee for the Republican ticket. In John McCain's own words: *"My friends and fellow Americans, I am very pleased and very privileged to introduce to you the next vice president of the United States — Gov. Sarah Palin of the great state of Alaska."* The news came as an all out assault on my senses. Like the piercing sound of the Emergency Broadcast System tone interrupting a beautiful cello piece, it jerked me into a reality that I wanted no part of. Please tell me this is a joke, I thought. But it didn't take long for the message to become real once I heard that VOICE...you know which one I mean...there is none like it...

I was faced with having to make a decision! "Quick, what do I do?"

In spite of my panic I immediately assessed that I really had only two options:

1) I could turn off every source of news and information, both visual and auditory, stay away from all printed media, and, for god's sake, do _not_ talk to any friends and family from Alaska – and calmly retreat to where I had been - in that moment of contentedness - before this incomprehensible news shattered my sense of all that was sane in the world; -_or_-

2) I could literally clear my desk, open up a new document and begin the cathartic process of writing about just how frightening this announcement truly was by alerting others about the deeper implications of choosing Palin as a national candidate and what I believed that it really meant - for all of us.

As you can see I chose the second option. I approached it with a passion that I had not felt politically in years since my days as a children and family issues lobbyist in Alaska. That level of passion can be exhausting, particularly when playing the game of political chess. I had convinced myself that it was okay to walk away, to drop out of that world and pretend that I could exist like so many people I have known throughout my life – the ones who are somehow capable of distancing themselves from politics, except for casting the obligatory vote now and again. What freedom, what calm, what bliss – I used to think – that these people must have, not paying attention to the political process, or watching how laws are _really_ made.

The announcement of Sarah Palin's nomination for Vice President of the United States was a surreal moment. Was my reaction to this news only because this woman was so clearly lacking in qualifications, world view and common sense? No. Did I believe for a moment that this was solely the brainstorm of John McCain? No. Was I concerned about how infested the Republican Party had become since the 1990s by religious zealots?

Absolutely! Did I see all this coming together before my eyes in an instant with the pick of Palin? *Oh, did I ever!*

Beyond her personal qualities, Palin stands for a dangerous trend in American politics. She is in the forefront of a decades-long effort to make this a Christian-only nation, even a theocracy in which only god's laws prevail. An agenda to capture the Constitution to empower Christian values, rights, and political dominance is coupled with a slate of "reforms" that would outlaw gains made over the past century in civil rights and racial equality. Those who seek an absolutist Christian control of America are Dominionists, and Sarah in 2008 was their voice, their candidate, their great hope. I feared the door she opened would be a floodgate for others. I was not wrong.

Next, as I watched what unfolded on that stage in Minneapolis, Minnesota at the 2008 Republican Convention where Palin gave her first national speech all I could think of was that this was a shot across the bow of religious and political freedom in America. Not that this hadn't been evident before when the Religious Right enjoyed its heyday, but this time the shot might as well be coming from a cannon rather than a rifle, the signs were that obvious. I was not alone in reading the warning signs and immediately embarked on research that included collaborating with a group of theological and political researchers across the country, which led me to write this book.

I am not an academic, nor a journalist, nor a politician. I am a fourth generation Alaskan, mother and grandmother. I am a former lobbyist for families and children, and I was raised in a politically conservative Christian Republican household; I understand politics. Having studied social psychology and personally experienced the wave of religious extremism that swept through Alaska as early as the 1960s, capturing some of my own family and friends in that tide. I am both an observer and an activist. I believe ardently that each and every one of us can make a difference *because I personally have.*

The real challenge remains: How do I get others to understand the significance of Palin's arrival onto our political landscape when she makes it so difficult to take her, and those like her, seriously?

2 Palin Fatigue

"I am not going to sit down, I am not going to shut up" ~ Sarah Palin January 18, 2011

We dodged a very, very close call in 2008 when Sarah Heath Palin splattered across our screens. As much as I would like to believe that we as a nation will ever let such an extreme and polarizing figure take the helm of our government, I cannot be certain. Because of that near miss, it is best that we all understand how this happened. We need to understand where she came from, how she got here, and what she is leaving behind in this tumultuous wake she has created. Palin isn't a "lone wolf;" there are and will be more like her. Understanding how she got here is crucial and helps us to see clearly how we can stop this from repeating itself.

If, at this very moment, Sarah Palin were to disappear suddenly into complete oblivion, it would not change the important lessons that surfaced when she catapulted to national and even international notoriety as the VP pick in 2008. She may go kicking and screaming, and many may not want to think about her for another moment, but the lessons are crucial.

Numerous times over the years, Palin has prided herself in saying she won't "sit down and shut up." Aside from every sane American wishing she would do just that, her own conservative puppetmasters called for her to pipe down by the time winter 2011 rolled around. Newt Gingrich made the following comment in January 2011 about Sarah Palin's uncontrollable verbal fits that emerged as a mish-mash of what has been aptly referred to as "word salad," *"I think that she's got to slow down*

*and be more careful and think through what she's
saying and how's she's saying it."*

The problem is she doesn't understand these
warnings and critiques even from those like Newt who
have their own problems refraining from making
outlandish statements in public. She views it rather as a
competitive attempt to quash her. One of the aspects of
this woman that will be discussed is Palin's devout
religious beliefs that feed her sense that she is on a
"mission" from god.

Palin believes that it is always about her –
anything and everything – and it is hard to argue that,
given the way she has been constantly thrust in our faces
in one form or another. When she has not intentionally
created her own attention-getting material, the queries go
out because she is too quiet. It is a love/hate relationship
with more people than are willing to admit it, and that
relationship extends beyond the borders of the United
States. Curiosity surrounding this women has been a
phenomenon.

I know this may come as a disappointment to
some, and a *huge* relief to most who read this – but this
book is about far more than simply Sarah Palin. It is
about the rise of extremism in America: religious, racist
and financial. God, guns and greed.

We watched extremism emerge as Palin traversed
the country igniting pockets of supporters across
America. These are the people who continue to support
her, and those like her: A population full of zealous, angry
extremists who see themselves as the "every-man" in
America. They believe they are in the majority and, from
the noise they make, the rest of us begin to believe they
are a majority right along with them.

Regardless of how you feel about Palin,
understanding how she was used to attract religious
conservative votes, will allow you to begin to see the
sense in all this. Since her announcement in 2008, Palin
has undeniably become one of the most recognizable

faces associated with uber-conservative politics in America. Her meteoric rise to political stardom demands that we acknowledge the impact she has had. This is true whether we are sick and tired of her and have already tuned out, or are morbidly glued to stories and "news" about Palin wondering where she will "go" next like watching an out-of-control train about to wreck.

This "every-man," or as Palin calls them, "rell Americans," vote – and if they do not cast their vote for her, it will be someone cut from the same cloth. The fact that she has enjoyed a favorable rating of *any* kind is yet another indicator that the Republican Party is threatened with extinction. Palin is the portal that gives us a look into the broader mess that has contributed to the division within the conservative population, a casting out of moderates and setting up ultra-conservative camps that are vying for control.

Her imposition into our world was, and is, the work of many factors. It is not just a knee-jerk reaction of one man. John McCain no more "picked" Sarah Palin to be his running mate than President Obama is a communist / fascist / socialist / Muslim (which, by the way, it would be impossible to be all at the same time). McCain knew full well that his campaign of 2008 was his last shot at running for the office of President of the United States and he was clearly willing to sell his soul to win. He had already reversed the politics of his recent past to generate the support and votes he knew he would need to get elected. By the time he was *told* that Palin would be on the ticket with him to secure the Christian conservative vote, he had already compromised whatever integrity he might have had in the prior years of his political career. What the hell? What was one more betrayal?

Was he happy about this choice? Let me put it this way: it didn't require a PhD in body language to recognize the overt signals of his total disdain for this woman who came from virtually nowhere and now sat next to him as his "equal," overshadowing him completely as she lapped up the limelight. Can you imagine his frustration? After all, he had paid his dues in a lifelong, hard-fought quest for the top leadership position in the world, and here she comes – and just waltzes in. It was no secret that McCain had a proven track record of disrespecting women and he wasn't about to embrace her on many levels. But, back in 2000, when he ran for president he called the Religious Right, "agents of intolerance" and that remark was now coming back to slap him upside the head. They never forgot and his 2008 handlers made the VP decision for him. As much as he wanted Joe Lieberman as his vice-president, he knew full well that he needed Palin. As much as he resented her, she was unavoidable were he to have even a chance to win.

The conundrum remains the same now as when they first picked her. They need her but do not like her. They also cannot ignore her or cast her aside completely because she continues to influence a segment of voters, and they need everyone of them.

So how did this happen? Who tapped her? How did she get here? And what in the hell were they thinking? We'll explore this because there are multiple answers. **IT IS SO MUCH MORE THAN SIMPLY A CONSERVATIVE POLITICAL MACHINE HAVING RUN AMOK.** It was a concerted effort by various interests all sporting their own agendas. A mixture, a batter of sorts, shall we say.

An American Recipe for Extremism ~ Homestyle

She is indeed the "Poster Gal" for this dangerous mixture. She has essentially taken one part Christian extremist, one part "Armed & Dangerous," and one part corporate and political greed run amok, and effectively stirred the powders of these divergent ideologies and emotions together into a mixture that cannot be separated, even if she wanted it to be (which she doesn't.)

God, Guns & Greed.

It's a three-part recipe for disaster; one that divides us and is leading us further and further into an environment where our freedoms are being extinguished by the very extremists who claim proprietary rights to them. Speech - Sovereignty - Free market.

3 We the *Real* People

The Perception of Politics

Fortunately, the good news is that the rest of us in America far outnumber those who fit the bill as extremists, and I am referring to both sides of the political pendulum. Both extremes manifest complete unwillingness to compromise. Both insist on remaining steadfastly in their perception that only they are "right." Both make a lot of noise, making it appear as if they are representing *all* of the rest of us in this nation. Well, *I beg to differ!*

For example, a New York Times poll revealed how Americans really felt about the "evil public option" after unparalleled heated debate in 2010. The question posed was, *"Would you favor or oppose the government offering everyone a government-administered health insurance plan like Medicare that would compete with private health insurance plans?"* And the answer was "65% favorable."

Perception: If you listen to the prognosticators on the political right you would think Americans are against what they mockingly refer to as "ObamaCare." Fact: Most Americans supported the major tenets of his health care legislation hands down. In fact, what these numbers tell us is that *most* Americans favored even stronger health care reforms than the bill that finally passed into law.

In that old adage, the squeaky wheel gets the grease –just because it makes the most noise. That doesn't mean, however that we have to buy that they are a real majority. –The vast majority in this country are more reasoned and take a more moderate view than all those noisemakers and pot-stirrers out there.

I truthfully have no appetite for extremism, no matter what or whose message it carries. I am often asked that if they are such a minority, then what do the rest of us look like if we are the majority? More of us are far more moderate in our lives, our faith, our politics and our worldviews than these fringe groups who pound their drums on both sides of the extremes.

As it happens, my publisher asked me that very question. I put together a list of sorts that includes most of us who I could describe as managing to view things - *moderately.*

Walkaways - Those who grew up in radical Christian theology known as Dominionism, and who came to recognize, for a myriad of reasons, that Dominionism is a sect, a bible-based cult and is purely unchristian. They see the signs and hear the zealous "codespeak" fall from the mouths of the likes of Perry, Palin, Huckabee, Bachmann, Pawlenty and others. They understand better than any of us just what these people represent in their push for a theocratic America.

Mainstream Christians - This group is often unfairly thrown into the same pool as the Dominionists and painted with the same brush. Elizabeth Sholes describes, *"Mainstream Protestants are a varied group, but we tend to be less focused on personal salvation and more on the teachings of Jesus. We want to make the world a far better place than we found it. We care about human equality, economic, political, and social justice, and providing good stewardship for the natural world. We speak from faith, but we speak for democracy. That's our centuries-old tradition that we reaffirm daily in the contemporary world."* The Dominionist Christians hold views that are virtually the opposite of Sholes' statement.

Castaways – These are politically secular Republicans who may hold strong religious views personally, yet believe in the separation of Church and State. Though fiscally conservative, they understand that de-regulation and privatization is simply a benefit to those who have proven that they have, and will, abuse those freedoms on the backs of the rest of us. These people were cast out of their own party in the late 1980s and early 1990s. They make up a sizeable portion of the registered "Independent" or "Nonpartisan" voters, and have the wherewithal to be appalled and embarrassed by the current incarnation of the Republican Party .

Moderate Republicans – This group is possibly the most frantic in their search for answers. They are growing increasingly uncomfortable with their fellow Party members, from the elected officials on down, yet cannot bring themselves to abandon their once cherished label of a proud Republican. They remain registered as "Rs" and were comfortable voting for McCain in 2008 right up until Sarah Palin joined the ticket. They still lend support to the GOP, but would never attend a Tea Party rally brandishing signs and certainly would never get behind and support loud-mouth entertainers like Rush Limbaugh as a "leader" of their Party. They are one step away from becoming "castaways."

Liberal/Progressives – Most often these are registered Democrats, but not always. While some in this group cling to a false sense of logic that Palin is a flash-in-the-pan narcissist who is operating independently and will never succeed in politics, once informed, many are moderate enough to listen to warning signs about the broader implications of the religio-political extremism side of Dominionist. These people tend to feel strongly about social justice.

Moderates – This group consists of those who are not necessarily loyal to any party, even though their voter registration card may state a party preference. This group has enough interest to register and vote, but they will not hold their noses and vote party lines whether liberal or conservative without reason. AS moderates, they appreciate that compromise is essential in our current political system.

24

Apolitical Americans – Typically unregistered citizens who state that *"They are all corrupt. I am not having anything to do with it!,"* when the subject of politics/politicians comes up. They tend to span across socio-economic lines but share a myopic view contained to their personal environment allowing them the delusion of an "us vs. them" mentality. These people are generally very comfortable focusing in on what directly impacts *them*, while completely ignoring that laws passed by those "corrupt" politicians impact all of us on local, state and federal levels. Yet even these political ostriches are rearing their heads to exclaim, "What the _hell_?" (when it comes to Palin and her ilk).

The Messenger ~ Rough Water and Huge Waves!

There are other groups that can be added to this list, but these are just a few that I have identified as I find my voice. By that I mean, whom am I trying to reach? As a messenger, I represent many, many people who have studied, researched and written about radical Christian politics in conservative America for years.

This book builds on that research along with my years of experience in politics, and is and enhanced further by my personal and family involvement with the religious movement that 'raptured' my mother right along with Palin's family (and millions of other Americans during the 60s and 70s) ultimately turning them into political foot soldiers for Christ.

There is simply so much information about this infestation of creeping theocracy that it can become overwhelming very quickly. So think of this as a primer, an introduction into this world that exists around us every day, yet seems to hide in plain sight.

Looking at the highly-organized and very well-funded movement behind Perry, Palin, Bachmann & Co. helps us to further understand Palin and the others. She was never a 'lone rogue' figure coming out of virtual obscurity who just happened to miraculously rocket to notoriety. This is *critical* in grasping why it is so necessary to learn *a bare minimum* about this woman. After all, she was thrust upon the rest of the world right along with all of us who call America our "home."

Ignore at our own peril ~ Even When Things Fall Silent

There are few certainties in this circus we call American politics but here are a couple that we can bank on regarding Palin.

This is absolutely critical: We must not make the mistake of thinking she simply sprung up out of nowhere, and

It is not only reckless, but irresponsible to continue to dismiss this woman as "irrelevant."

We hear it from paid "in-the-know" political pundits, both liberal and conservative, that she is not a serious force to be reckoned with. I have political friends – in Alaska, no less – who have repeatedly told me that very line. "Palin's yesterday's news!" they say. "She's irrelevant, no one is going to take her seriously!" while they roll their eyes at me, rejecting my concerns.

What do I say to that? For me, as long as "we" are still talking about her, as long as she continues to grab headlines through her Facebook and ridiculous tweets, and as long as this woman continues to weasel and wrangle every ounce of attention possible she will remain very relevant. Why, you ask? Because, this is no longer just about whether or not Palin ever has the opportunity to measure for drapes in the Oval office, let alone have access to the "nucular" codes (and yes, she "relly" does say it just like George Bush did). Rather, it is because she did rise to a level of nuisance and notoriety that now requires us to be here, having this discussion.

If this woman disappeared into the Arctic wilds today, her arrival in 2008 forever contributed to an uncivil shift in political discourse in American politics. This shift has contributed to a member of Congress thinking it appropriate to shout, "Liar!" in the middle of a speech by the President of the United States of America on the floor of Congress. People suddenly began to take loaded weapons to Town Hall meetings even when it was to hear the President speak, in order to flex their Second Amendment rights (even though their rights were not threatened). Fights broke out in public meetings and elected officials were booed and screamed at when trying to hold debates about health care reform in America.

Beyond any political ambitions that Palin may have, and whether any of those ambitions become successful, it is what she has and will continue to bring to the religious-conservative political table that is of grave concern for us all. It is unprecedented that if this woman so much as makes a remark via a social media account, it is then picked up by the media worldwide and discussed as news. Her carefully edited FOX appearances are replayed across the spectrum hitting every conceivable media source, permeating our airwaves. This is irrefutable. It is not just that she is covered by the media – it is how they cover her.

For as long as she garners attention like a vacuum sucking the oxygen out of the room – she remains relevant.

For as long as she is able to energize and motivate many in extreme right politics in America - she remains relevant.

For as long as she empowers and promotes other politicians just like her, winning at any cost – she remains relevant.

For as long as she is able to incentivize the anti-government fringe by feeding them a constant diet of fear and paranoia and calls for revolution – she remains relevant.

27

Palin Plays Persecution Politics Perfectly

Maintaining the appearance of constant persecution by the "lamestream media" and those liberal elites takes effort, time and co-ordination, but the pay-off is substantial. Not only does she remain planted in the media, but one way or another, the reason for the persecution is somehow always brought back to Palin's devotion to her religious belief. Therefore, to pick on her makes you anti-American and subsequently anti-Christian.

The "persecution as a Christian" meme is intentional and it works. There are numbers spewed out to Americans as fact stating that Christians suffer higher incidences of persecution than any other religious group in America. Is it true? No. Do the facts matter? Not even remotely, as we will see throughout this discussion. All that matters is the perception and Palin & Co. are becoming quite adept at this game. Without fail, every single time it appears that she is under attack and/or criticized, (largely for her own actions, by the way), her base rallies with even more fervent rancor and vitriol.

Sarah Palin is a "born again" zealot who absolutely, unequivocally fully intends to do all that she can to marry Church & State whether that is as an elected official or from the outside. Palin and those like her push others to prepare for the Second Coming of Christ, and this begins with our three branches of government: The Congress, The White House and the Supreme Court. Sound alarming? It is, and I am really not an alarmist.

Remember, Perry, Palin Bachmann & Company all fundamentally hope to regulate social morals through legislation, privatize government and nationalize their religion. All of these would be imposed on us at the cost of our freedoms

Before we go further let's take a look at the environment from which she came. It resembles many areas across America where others like her are embedding their religious views into politics. Make no mistake: In spite of the "Alaska" in her address, she is a "Bible-belt" American.

Palin was raised in an area of Alaska that can be compared to "Anytown, USA." I know that will offend some who live in the Matanuska-Susitna (Mat-Su) Valley of Alaska where Wasilla is located, but it is not meant to. The plain truth is that she did not live in the rough and wilds of the wilderness. She was raised with nearby convenience stores, shopping malls, traffic lights and four-lane highways. Perspective is needed here to override the romanticized origins of Sarah Palin. There is no arguing that part of what sold this woman to the rest of the world is the appeal of Alaska a state filled with rugged pioneers. This actually does apply to a handful of those who migrated north to Alaska over the years, but now-a-days only to a very few, and Palin is not one of them..

Let me put it this way: If Sarah Palin had been from Decatur, Indiana, you would never have heard her name..

Sorry, Sarah...reality bites.

4 Tale of Two Alaskas

"North to the Future" - "The Last Frontier"
    Alaska's Official State Motto
    & Nickname

...And northward they came.

I am going to start with some Alaska history that is really not as different from the rest of the United States as some would like to portray it. Without a doubt, it t does have a unique twist, but the similarities are noteworthy.

Like so many other immigrants over the centuries, people were motivated to head to Alaska to capitalize on the vast resources offered by its land and sea, and to seek the isolation that such a vast land mass has to offer. Some of these groups included:

European explorers in the 17th and 18th centuries who sailed the coastline as fur traders;

Russians who staked settlement claims to Alaska in the mid-18 to 19th centuries;

A flood of people stricken with "gold fever" who suffered unspeakable hardships (many of whom perished) in their quest for wealth in the Yukon and Nome gold rush of the 1890s, and;

A modern-day "black gold" rush of the 1960s when one of the world's largest oil discoveries was made in Prudhoe Bay, Alaska on its most northern Arctic shore.

All of these waves of immigrants left their mark on Alaska. In addition, of course, there is an indigenous native population, who were the original settlers arriving in Alaska centuries before the first "white man" arrived.

But what do they all have in common? All are immigrants. Each and every one of us at one point migrated to Alaska seeking something. My maternal ancestors came by ship from Scandinavia, drawn to Alaska for her homeland geographical similarities to their homeland, as well as their vision of the mysteries and opportunities that would lie ahead.

Many came as fishers, miners, loggers and for the pure draw of becoming a "pioneer," as the myths of Alaska spread across the "Lower 48', piquing interest in ever-growing numbers. Growing up there we were frequently asked by "lower 48" friends and relatives if we "lived in igloos," "ate whale blubber" and or had year-round snowfall. Nearly fifty years later there are still people in the United States who wonder about these things. (By the way, the answer to all three is "no.") Alaska remains a place of mystery for most people with its varied cultures and incredible landscape, which range from the fjords and glaciers in Southeast Alaska, to the highest peak in North America, Mt. McKinley; to the enormous uninhabited miles of land and shoreline.

This interest is precisely why Sarah Palin draws more curiosity than she would have had her family remained in Sandpoint, Idaho where she was born. If Palin had risen from obscurity as a mom from Topeka, Kansas or Dubuque, Iowa or Canton, Ohio (well, you get the idea),the interest in her would not have come *close* to what it was. If this were not the case, Michele Bachmann could well have been chosen as McCain's vice presidential candidate Bachmann is virtually Palin's political twin with, in the summer of 2008, a longer political resume. But Alaska gets attention and draws people in – and Palin & Co. know this. This is marketing.

Much of the fascination and intrigue with this woman lies in the fact that she sells herself as a "pioneer Alaskan," a stretch as long as an Alaskan mile!

There continues to exist today a persistent fascination by people from around the world as to just what they might see or experience on a visit to this unique State. They come by sea, by air and by land. You have only to witness the popularity of the Alaska cruise industry as the massive ships sail through the tiny ports, often completely dwarfing the local community that they are visiting, to see firsthand the enormity of this interest.

As anywhere, migrations of people always change the landscape of the environment around them. The discovery of one of the world's largest oil fields happened not only *in* Alaska but *to* Alaska.

What has occurred in Alaska in the past forty years, since the discover of oil, both physically and socially, is a story that explains just how a person such as Sarah Palin can emerge seemingly out of nowhere, and onto a national political stage, sold as champion of the "common folk."

Interest in Alaska existed prior to Sarah Palin becoming a recognizable name, and it has increased exponentially as she has continued to generate attention. My experience of "growing up Alaskan" in mostly pre-oil discovery days and in communities all across this vast State, contrasts significantly with the experience of those that grew up in the post-oil discovery cities and towns of Alaska that Sarah Palin is from.

There are as many misconceptions about Alaska as there are wonders. The temptation is great to embellish and exaggerate aspects of what it was like to grow up in this unique state, or what it is like to live there. Take, for instance, the Hollywood fantasy of the Palins' everyday lives portrayed in the Learning Channel's, eight-episode series, titled, *"Sarah Palin's Alaska."* Here is a perfect example of embellishment on reality to keep the lure alive with those who like stories of real life heroines. But alas, a heroine she is not. She is also not a hunter-gatherer, an outdoorsy gal, an America's personification of the perfect mom, a seasoned politician, and most importantly not "just one of the people."

She *is* however, by her own admission, definitely not an "elite." Having actually been raised in Alaska I can attest that growing up there looks entirely different from the picture conjured up in the minds of most Americans. These myths, though interesting, are as numbered as the truths from igloos and polar bears around every corner, to darkness 24/7.

And then let's not forget the political myths! These are real doosies! More on those shortly...

Sourdoughs vs. Cheechakos

The bulk of today's population in the State of Alaska can really be considered "Cheechakos," and the minority are "Sourdoughs." A *Cheechako* is a newcomer, or a "tenderfoot," and a *Sourdough* is an old-timer or veteran Alaskan, sometimes called a "true" Alaskan. The state is so young that hardly anyone has had time to develop much history outside of the Alaska natives who migrated there centuries ago. Nonetheless, there are a handful of us who are non-native that can claim a longer than average history in this unusual state. My family came to Alaska (on my mother's side) four generations ago, and our heritage is primarily Scandinavian.

As recently as the 1960s, residents faced challenges that didn't exist for most Americans such as the cost and availability of our food supply. But with the constant advances in transportation of goods, Alaska has become a true sibling of the United States, resembling her family *"down south,"* (considered to include ALL of the 48 contiguous states).

Palin and I grew up in different versions of Alaska. My experience can be contrasted with Sarah Palin's as a statewide versus community-centered experience.

For example, her family moved from Idaho and settled into an area which saw significant population growth due to the increasing migration of oilfield workers who came to Alaska from *"Outside."* (This is another term used by Alaskans to describe those from the *"Lower 48",*). These immigrants brought with them ideologies and values that differed from their new surroundings. Because they never assimilated into their new communities, these communities were transformed to resemble *them* rather than the other way around.

No matter where we live, change occurs, and we all have our Sourdoughs and Cheechakos. Whether you reside in a small town, out in rural farm country, in the heart of a city or out on an island, all of us know what it is like to function within a small community. Even in large cities people will tend to divide into sub-communities, and then sub-sub-communities. All of us can truly relate to what it is like to live in a "small town" on some level.

Close the Borders and Pull Up the Ramp!

Beginning in the late 1960s, there was a significant surge in the state's population. Most of these immigrants originated from the oilfield Gulf States such as Louisiana, Oklahoma and Texas. Once in Alaska, a majority of these oilfield workers settled in and around Fairbanks, Anchorage, the Kenai Peninsula south of Anchorage, and to the west in what is known as the "Mat-Su Valley." Mat-Su is short for Matanuska-Susitna which is a borough (equivalent to "county" in most other states) about the size of the State of West Virginia and includes several communities. Some of the Mat-Su communities include Wasilla, Palmer, Willow, and Houston. These towns are all less than an hour drive on a four lane highway from the sprawling metropolitan city of Anchorage.

Anchorage, with a population pushing 300,000 is as modern and thriving as most cities in the United

States. It offers experiences, services and atmosphere rivaling most areas in the America, and is about as far from the pioneering Alaskan experience as one can get. In fact, this is where the majority (about 40%) of Alaskans live. It is a rare non-native who chooses to live in a self-imposed pioneering manner of isolation and subsistence, and it is always by *choice*. Believe me, you do not need to be "Annie Oakley" to put dinner on the table – another one of those myths.

Many of these Cheechakos originated from not only the Gulf States, but those states traditionally referred to as the "Bible-belt" of America. They brought their religious and world views, their "values" if you will. They are predominantly very conservative and their churches are very restrictive in their views basing much of their dogma in the Old Testament. This is evident in how they talk about the roles of women, men and children, defined in accordance with their *version* of biblical values.

Sarah Palin's family qualifies as one of thousands of immigrants who came north in the 1970s and took up roots in the Mat-Su. Rather than becoming "Alaskan," they remained who they were, and continued to exist in *that* culture, with the reality and ideologies that they brought with them to Alaska, though miles from their origins.

Alaska had recently become a new state with much to offer but many of these newcomers came with a desire to change it, rebelling against its land use, hunting and fishing laws, squatter's rights and more. They even took it to another level and collectively assembled in concerted efforts to take the State down the path of reverting its newfound statehood. They still cry for secession. We had *just* become a member of the Union of the United States of America in 1959, literally nine years before the discovery of oil in Alaska, and these newly arrived folks had their eyes set on undoing the State of Alaska and laying claim to the vast resources the State had to offer for their very own. (*There will be more about one of these specific organizations in the section about the Alaska Independence Party.*) For now, this story is noteworthy in depicting from what type of environment Palin emerged.

Understanding where she came from and more about the environment she was raised in helps us to counter the fabricated image that we see today. She has absolutely experienced an unprecedented rocket-ride to notoriety with this contrived image, which serves to mask the realities of what formed her as an individual.

Sarah Palin was raised in a modern community, with a full array of modern conveniences, goods and media. Understanding this, as well as understanding her religious upbringing is essential to understanding Sarah.

Palin's Alaska Through Biblical Glasses ~ God's Country

Back in the late 1970s I actually worked in the Prudhoe Bay oil-field. I lived there for two years and many of the blue-collar line workers that I encountered daily on the "Slope (*referring to the North Slope of Alaska in Prudhoe Bay where the oil comes out of the ground and the camps are located*) when I worked there were neighbors of Sarah's. They held to a very conservative world view, which was dramatically different by comparison to what I had been exposed to growing up from shore to shore in Alaska.

I was raised where there existed not an entrenched conservative population, but a large contingent of registered "Independent." A "live and let live" attitude resonated among both the liberals and conservatives in Alaska back then. In its early days, the majority (meaning who held more elected seats in the Alaska Legislature) swung back and forth between both major parties. But since the 1970s it can be said without question that

Alaska has politically become an ever-increasingly deep, deep, red state politically, and it is a shade of red painted with a religious brush.

Additionally, the ideas and attitudes that were emerging in the 70s and 80s had to do with an almost paranoid fear of interference from the government, especially where their families were concerned. For example, I was told by one Mat-Su resident in the late 1980s that "<u>no</u> one was going to tell *them* how they could discipline their wives and children," during a debate about child abuse legislation. In fact, one of their very own elected officials, Representative Jeannette James from North Pole (*Okay, that is one of those myths that is actually true – there really IS a North Pole, Alaska*), a neighboring community to Fairbanks, unapologetically shared this lilting remark as her opening statement in a Health, Education & Social Services Committee that she was Chairing,

"It is better that one child continue to be abused – than one family falsely accused."

It was during this time period, and over these social issues, that I first encountered Palin and her congregation over the battle of abortion procedures at the Mat-Su Valley Hospital. I was a lobbyist at that time working to oppose their efforts to pass legislation that would require a girl to get parental consent before seeking an abortion. On the surface this argument sounds reasonable, but there are many reasons why this poses a threat to the young woman. Suffice it to say that we were on opposite sides of this issue where I was arguing for the safety of the mother and their concerns were solely on the undeveloped fetus.

For them this was (and is) a zero gray area. It was purely black and white. What solace it must provide to live in a world where you can claim such absolutes and dictate them to everyone else' lives, to be so resolute, so sanctimonious in their belief, all the while making these life-changing judgments and decisions, not just for themselves -but for the rest of us. They insist that we adhere to their religious worldview whether we like it or not. This is where much of Palin's early formation came, in a world of zealous passion for Palin, surrounded by people who saw nothing amiss in imposing their religion on the rest of us - even if it meant ramming it down our throats through legislation.

This was the new culture that was moving into Alaska and pounding down their roots. People who, though touting themselves as "good honest god-fearin' 'Mericans," displayed a world depleted of a compassionate social attitude. It was more of an "all for one" view; either you are viewed as with us or against us.

This is the Alaska that Sarah Heath Palin grew up in during the 1970s and 1980s.

In Search of the "Bubblin' Crude" ~ A Pilgrimage

After a certain point, it became clear that not only were they not leaving, they were here to stay, Bible-belt world view and all. These "new" Alaskans not only imported their ideas but even *more* people from Outside. The pilgrimage aspect of this migration, and that these folks are still encouraged to this day to attract increasing numbers to flood north. is an ongoing dynamic. This no longer has anything to do with oil, at least not crude oil It is more like the Wesson oil they use for anointing.

As I said earlier, I really do understand that change happens everywhere, but this was, until that time, a state that held conservative fiscal views along with compassionate social values by not only its liberals, but its "conservatives" as well. There was agreement in appreciation for secular government and an overarching embrace of the sense of community that spanned the entire state. Because we had such a small population to begin with, this type of migration had profound impacts, and the shifts that ultimately occurred in Alaska ,politically and socially ,were, and are noticeable and long-lived.

Suddenly, the State was inundated with people pouring in, looking for their claim to wealth, not unlike those gold rushers of the 1890s. Full page newspaper ads were placed in papers across the country that appealed to workers to "go north." Word spread that you could get a job on the pipeline with little to no experience or education and earn anywhere from $1,000-$5,000 per week as starting pay. In the 1970s, with the minimum wage less than $3.00 per hour, this was a staggering sum. You can imagine the excitement!

Reality was a much different story and the number of available job openings were drastically less than the huge number of people seeking one of these lofty paychecks. Not only that, but those coming North were, in many cases, woefully ill-prepared in terms of money, shelter or knowledge of the vastness of Alaska. The distance from the southernmost community, Ketchikan, to the town that did most of the interviewing for pipeline employment, Fairbanks, is 1,000 miles, but actual travel distance there, if not by plane, was hundreds more. This is similar to travelling from Seattle to Los Angeles; or from Washington, D.C. to Miami, Florida. Without an appreciation for these distances people made crucial mistakes in planning. Once you have encountered the sign that says "Welcome to the Last Frontier" you may or may not be even remotely close to your destination. You could be many, many hundreds of miles from where you needed to go or thought you were going.

This became a significant problem . Many who had sold all that they owned, quit their jobs, packed up their vehicles and families and charged north for one of those high-paying pipeline jobs found themselves not coming within hundreds of miles of the pipeline. Instead, they were broke, stranded and unable to return home. I personally remember quite well the toll this influx of people was having on our communities. Some of it was costly to our infrastructure as well as our sense of peace and security.

We began experiencing homeless people sleeping in their cars and makeshift shelters because they had not calculated the costs and the distances in Alaska. They'd come to Alaska with no job, just the belief that they would get one. Crimes increased including break-ins and people literally "squatting" in homes that may have only been temporarily empty by a vacationing owner. Suddenly, these out of work newcomers found themselves at the base of the "black gold" rainbow with no money, resources or a back-up plan. They were at the end of the trail.

It became so dire that it was necessary to post an Alaska State Trooper at the southern most terminal for the Alaska State Ferry System in Seattle, Washington who was charged with demanding that people produce a minimum amount of money before being allowed to travel north. The point of that was to make sure they at least had enough to get to where they were going and hopefully get themselves back. Alaska was burdened with the care of this migration as the state experienced a drain on its services from unemployment to health care.

The number of people moving into Alaska who actually secured employment added to the number of those who became stranded and could not find employment; this made for a significant population boom. According to U.S. Census data, Alaska experienced a 78% - yes, *a seventy-eight percent* – growth in population between 1960 and 1980 "due exclusively to the migration of workers spanning the pipeline construction phase in the oil industry."

Alaska's days of tolerating differences were coming to a swift end and none of us were prepared for, nor understood the magnitude of, what the bigger picture would be. This state was young and changes were happening rapidly! Remember, we had only been a State for nine years when oil was discovered, so the shifts were dramatic.

And again, *this* is the environment in which Sarah Palin grew to adulthood.

Pre-Oil Boom Days

I was born in a very different Alaska in the fall of 1957, in the town of Ketchikan on Revillagigedo Island in the southernmost panhandle of the state. Some of you may recognize the name of this tiny community - Ketchikan – which received its "fifteen minutes of fame" when Palin became the 2008 Republican vice presidential nominee because of the debate about funding the "bridge to nowhere." This was an actual bridge project that would have cost an estimated 398 million federal dollars that Palin initially supported, yet later became famous for her "Thanks, but no thanks!" version of opposing the bridge project. Then-Republican Senator Ted Stevens (now deceased) also supported this spending and was responsible for almost bringing home the pork for this project. Kinda shoots holes in the anti-earmark rhetoric we hear from Palin and her ilk, doesn't it?

Ketchikan still proudly displays their "welcome" sign that greets everyone with, *"Welcome to Alaska's 1st City – Ketchikan – The Salmon Capital of the World."* They aren't kidding, for at one time it was just that, the salmon capital, with a vibrant economy and a flourishing fishing and logging industry. Now, due to fewer resources available to support those industries, Ketchikan has become almost exclusively relegated to the business of catering to tourism as its primary income base. This has happened in nearly every port town in Alaska that has been put on the cruise circuit. Local small business owners lose out as the franchise-ready remodels swoop in, opening the very same shops that sell T-shirts and jewelry anywhere these ships sail worldwide. "Old Alaska" is becoming unrecognizable.

I grew up as the second oldest of four siblings. My father's first job was working on the crews that prepped sections of Alaska's then all-dirt roads for paving. His work eventually took him to Ketchikan where he met and married my mother in 1954 before joining the Ketchikan Police Department, launching his life-long career in Alaska law enforcement, from which he retired in 1994 as Commissioner of Public Safety. He served as Commissioner in the Cabinets of two of Alaska's Republican governors, Governor Walter J. Hickel and Governor Jay S. Hammond (both deceased).

Once Dad joined the Alaska State Police our family was off and moving, as nomadic as any native tribe in search of sustenance, shelter and livelihood. Alaska was only a year-old as a State when he first went to work for it and there were many state employee policies that had not even been created yet. One of those policies that had yet to be established was how frequently it was reasonable to uproot state employee families and move them around. As a result we "served" right along with Dad, at the will and judgment of the current administrations' interpretation of "need" for the various communities. We literally moved so many times that my mother admittedly lost count, and I couldn't tell you with accuracy how many times myself.

Our destinations were varied and spread throughout the entire state of Alaska including remote villages such as Dillingham (where Todd Palin's family comes from) in the Bristol Bay Region where my little brother was born. We were sent from the frozen and dark winter-world of Fairbanks up in the northern interior to a couple of years in the big metropolitan sprawl known as Anchorage where we had our first house, real honest-to-god TV, stores and gas stations... and timing that put us squarely in the throes of the famous Anchorage earthquake which tossed central Alaska on Good Friday

March 27th, 1964. (That quake remains the largest disturbance of its kind recorded on the North American continent at a whopping 9.2 on the Richter Scale.) I was convinced that it was the end of the world because my mother had read Children's Bible Stories to us so many times and the Book of Revelations depicted the end as the "mountains will crumble."

My mother was a third generation Alaskan, born in Ketchikan in 1934 where she eventually lived out her life. Because my father's job took us all over the state and subjected us to many different and very challenging living conditions, my mother worked hard in her effort to provide my three siblings, my father and me with some semblance of "home" as we were transferred from place to place.

The hardships were countless and my parents essentially had parallel lives in a great many ways. My father was responsible for keeping the peace in areas where inciting a bar brawl with the lone local cop was the high-light of the weekends' entertainment for some rabble-rousers, whether they were fishermen, loggers or natives. In extreme cases, hauling someone "in" literally could mean a plane ride for hundreds of miles to the nearest jail and court system, and it could be days before he would return home. His job was difficult in many aspects. However, he clearly enjoyed it in other ways as evidenced when he would come home after a good romp with the local color, glasses askew, uniform patches in need of re-adhering, and a smile on his face.

Mom's reality was not so enjoyable. She had to pull things together sometimes out of nothing. Resources were very limited back then, and I am not just referring to income. There was a lack of available products in many of the places we lived. This included food, clothing, and other relatively common household conveniences. We were lucky to have a Sears or a Montgomery Ward's catalog store nearby in a *few* of the towns we lived in from which to order (when we could afford it.) Otherwise, mom made all our clothes. I hated wearing homemade clothes, but in hindsight not only was that the best my parents could do, but at least I got my sister's hand-me-downs. My little brothers got ours! Poor little guys...

Mom came from a Scandinavian family that came to Southeast Alaska in the 1800s. My grandparents were caretakers of the Sunny Point Cannery in Ketchikan until my grandfather retired in the 1980s. You didn't have to live in the villages for life to be challenging in this new place and people either loved it or hated it. I admit that, depending on the topic, I could go either way with those emotions. I grew up with many harsh realities: The very long winters, with extremely little daylight for one-third to two-thirds of the year (depending on where you live); the distances that one has to travel; the expense for basic necessities; the lack of access to activities and events that were routinely taken for granted in the Lower 48.

I remember, due to bitter cold and virtually no insulation in an outpost at which we were stationed, my mother mopping the kitchen floor and watching a thin film of ice form on it before it even had a chance to dry. At times, we all had to sleep in the same room for warmth! I remember real dogsleds, snowshoes and watching native women make our mukluks (boots) and mittens as they chewed the hide with their teeth, molding the soles and then sewing on the fur. (I won't even tell you what they soaked the hide in before putting them in their mouths and then chewing on the hide to soften them; trust me, you don't want to know.)

My father would check our school bus stops for bears or other predatory animals in the morning. The only milk I knew growing up was powdered milk mixed with canned because there was no fresh milk – ever. In several of the communities where we lived, my mother had only a couple of opportunities each year to submit her list for canned goods and products in order to meet the deadline of the next fishing fleet or barge that was heading south and would return from Seattle, weeks later, with these goods.

I also remember amazing and wonderful things: Dark winters and bright summers, the thunderous sounds of the Mendenhall glacier "calving" (the term for huge chunks of ice falling off the face of a glacier), and watching magnificent displays of the northern lights dance in the sky. The entire state felt like one big town. It was hard to travel to any corner of it and not run into people that you either knew directly or knew someone in common. There was a real sense of community and camaraderie.

I also remember the discovery of oil, the onset of the pipeline days, the migration of a Bible-belt population and, suddenly how everyone was clamoring to get a piece of the pie.

I remember how everything changed.

5 Name It & Claim It

Religion is *the* single most important aspect of this whole discussion. Religion, particularly an extreme sect of Christianity, has played an ever-increasing role in the shaping of our communities in Alaska. In this, Alaska is no different than other parts of America and the world as they strong-arm their way into people's lives and different cultures. Theirs in the only "way, truth and light" of every living being on the earth whether you agree or not.

In my family, we were raised and baptized in the Lutheran Church. My mother was a devout Christian even before my father turned to the church. Mom's faith began to emerge when we lived out in Bristol Bay. She would spend time with two women in particular who I later found out were missionaries. They would occasionally take my mother on outings, sometimes flying off in a little single prop airplane to nearby places like across Kvichak Bay to Naknek and King Salmon to beach comb. It was from her relationship with these women and others at the local church in Dillingham, that she was swept up in the evangelical wave that began to pick up speed in Alaska as early as the 1960s.

I have a distinct memory of her stating that she had been "born-again;" "saved" she told me. This memory is so clear to me because at age six I wondered, "If you are already born, how can you be *born again*?" And saved from what? Mom's re-birth in Christ was near the same time when my youngest brother was born and my view of birth was pretty specific, or so I thought. At that time we were attending the local Church of Christ.

We were faithful church-goers and it was clear that the church was the answer for her and comforted her during difficult times so she never understood it when I began questioning the hypocrisy I witnessed. Bad behavior during the week by fellow church members seemed easily swept away by the act of simply attending Sunday services the following week. I never lost my belief in God, but it did take a philosophical turn away from adhering to the literal views that my mother clung to.

I did not turn my back on Christianity. It was just that it became increasingly more evident to me that so much of what was being proclaimed in *the name of God* was more of a benefit to man, and more precisely to the small percentage of men at the top who were scripture-twisting the Bible to suit their need for control of the congregations. Our current rise of uber-conservative Christianity has done nothing but re-enforce that very perspective – leaving me to ask, in whose name are they doing their deeds? Jesus or "GEEzus!"

There was a wave of Christianity that swept the state, beginning in the late 1960s. I not only watched it happen, but my mother coordinated with kids of families I grew up around to trick me into attending a revival that was coming to town one year. These kids and their families were now professed "born-agains" which requires the act of renouncing your baptism at birth in exchange for having a "born-again" birth date. It was a requirement to be accepted into this new religious movement, yet I could not reconcile all that pomp and circumstance with my own views of Christianity. (Note: It was during this same period that the Palins, like so many other Alaska residents became evangelical Christians).

The revival, by the way, was a performance by David Wilkerson who was on tour promoting his new book at that time called, *"The Cross & the Switchblade."*

Mr. Wilkerson was a conservative religious extremist who died April 27th, 2011. He was quite successful at "harvesting the souls" of many in his audiences that shook, gyrated, convulsed and spoke in gibberish or "glossolalia," better known as speaking in tongues.

The hair on the back of my neck went up as I witnessed a high school auditorium in Ketchikan that was full of young people, many of whom I knew, get raptured into the energy that Wilkerson was manufacturing on that stage. It did not take me long to simply walk away from this "show," but I did so with a very uneasy feeling as so many of the kids I had grown up with were entranced by the whole spectacle, glassy eyes and all. This was Wilkerson's first stop as his revival performance worked its way north to other communities including Anchorage.

This was 1973 and Sarah Palin was only nine years old at the time and still being raised as a Catholic.

The Evangelical Conference that Changed the "Mission"

It was 1974 in a place called Lausanne, Switzerland where a gathering happened that brought together nearly 2,700 evangelical Christian leaders for a ten-day conference that is touted as creating "one of the most influential documents in evangelical Christianity." One very notable American preacher, Billy Graham, was on the committee that called for the conference. This event established the "Lausanne Committee for World Evangelization" and off they went, racing to all corners of the earth with special focus on "first nations" people.

In Alaska that meant the Alaskan native population. But along with this dedication to evangelizing and converting indigenous peoples was an all out competition to convert or "harvest" (their language not mine) as many souls as possible for Jesus.

48

The Palins were not the only ones to succumb to this movement as it set up shop in Alaska in the 1970s and grew rapidly in the coming years. It is significant to know that Sarah Palin's family switched their allegiance of faith from the Catholic Church to the Dominionist Movement during this very period in a time that so many were professing a "born again" transformation in their lives. This transition had dramatic effects for many Christians. I was there, I felt it, I saw it and I experienced it around me.

Sarah Palin's religious views grew out of this wave of evangelicalism, and her dedication to her faith is an issue because she has made it one. She claims to not make a move without direction (as she has stated) from divine guidance. This is seriously problematic when a person such as Palin and others like her then set their eyes on national political office. As far back as November 10th, 2008 she began feeding her message to an audience that now extended beyond the borders of Alaska:

> *You know, I have -- faith is a very big part of my life. And putting my life in my Creator's hands -- this is what I always do. I'm like, OK, God, if there is an open door for me somewhere, this is what I always pray, I'm like, don't let me miss the open door. Show me where the open door is. Even if it's cracked up a little bit, maybe I'll plow right on through that and maybe prematurely plow through it, but don't let me miss an open door. And if there is an open door in '12 or four years later, and if it is something that is going to be good for my family, for my state, for my nation, an opportunity for me, then I'll plow through that door. - as told to Greta Van Susteren of FOX infotainment.*

"Name It & Claim It" is <u>exactly</u> what they did!

The process of "Name it & Claim It" is an actual practice performed in ritual by these religious zealots. It is referred to in many ways including the "Prosperity Gospel." Here is an excerpt from a study called, "The Bankruptcy of the Prosperity Gospel" by David Jones at Bible.org:

> *This gospel has been ascribed many names, such as the "name it and claim it" gospel, the "blab it and grab it" gospel, the "health and wealth" gospel, the "word of faith" movement, the "gospel of success," the "prosperity gospel," and "positive confession theology."*
>
> *No matter what name is used, though, the teaching is the same. Simply put, this egocentric gospel teaches that God wants believers to be materially wealthy. Listen to the words of Robert Tilton, one of the prosperity gospel's most well-known spokesmen: "I believe that it is the will of God for all to prosper because I see it in the Word [of God], not because it has worked mightily for someone else. I do not put my eyes on men, but on God who gives me the power to get wealth."*
>
> *Teachers of the prosperity gospel encourage their followers to pray, and even demand, of God "everything from modes of transportation (cars, vans, trucks, even two-seat planes), [to] homes, furniture, and large bank accounts.*

Name it and claim it is a "theology" taught by some televangelists, faith healers, and Pentecostal preachers.

Some of them think the "name it and claim it" label is derogatory and prefer it be called "Word of Faith" or the "prosperity gospel."

The gist of "name it and claim it" is that the Bible contains numerous promises from God to Christian believers, but that believers have to first "claim" the promise before it can become effective. These "promises" may include healing from disease, exorcism of evil spirits, power to engage in Spiritual Warfare against Satan, or various supernatural gifts supposedly from the Holy Spirit. This is also how they view territories, as in actual named pieces of land, and the Dominionists have done this to Alaska in the name of GEEzus!

Below is a short list of those who preach this extremism:

    Todd Bentley

    Kenneth Copeland

    Paul Crouch

    Creflo Dollar

    Kenneth Hagin

    Benny Hinn

    Bob Larson (claims not to promote it, but does)

    Eddie Long

    Joel Osteen (makes me feel "warm inside")

    Pat Robertson (has attempted this practice on a grander scale by ordering hurricanes to change their course in the name of Jesus)

This is where getting rich is not in conflict with their beliefs. Many people say about Palin, *"It's not her religion! She is just out to get rich!"* Well, I am here to tell you that it is *both*! For Sarah Palin, getting rich is part of her religion. Personal wealth is not only not inconsistent with her religious view, but it is seen as directly correlating with faith. The more successful you are, the more faith you have. If you fail to understand this, you miss an essential starting point in understanding Dominionism.

6 Growing up Together

"The Last Frontier"

As I indicated above, I was born in 1957 when Alaska was still a territory, two years before it became a state in 1959. We have really grown up together. Because Alaska was so young and comes second only to Wyoming in the least number of people residing in a state, it was not unusual to have people you knew well be the same people who'd been instrumental in creating the system under which Alaska still lives.

I have had the experience of meeting those who signed Alaska's Constitution, and those who wrote the first guidelines for introducing legislation and the passage of bills. I witnessed those efforts culminate in written regulations establishing procedural guidelines for departments and the management of Alaska's government.

Being involved in politics not only gave me a working knowledge of the Alaska political system but the privilege of knowing many of its cast of what can often times be referred to as honest-to-god characters. I continue to enjoy close ties to friends in political office and other positions of involvement in Alaska's political arena who are committed to working for the future good of the "Last Frontier."

Politics is challenging in such a vast state with a sparse population. Even though it has grown from 228,000 in the 1960s to a reported 2008 count of 686,293, it is still only comparable to a city the size of Memphis, Tennessee; Baltimore, Maryland; Ft. Worth Texas or Charlotte, North Carolina. This "small town feel" to the state allowed for unusual access to its political process and exposure to politics Alaska-style. My access was greatly increased due in large part to my father's political involvements and contacts.

In my youth he took me where most could not go. I explored the governor's mansion when he was in charge of protection for the governor(s), and meandering significant portions of the Capitol Building where he had an office at one point in the 1960s, back when most of Alaska's government was housed in this single building.

At that time I could not have imagined that in the years to come I would "play" in those same buildings and hallways as an adult and professional lobbyist, researching, preparing and refining my persuasive arguments in attempt to persuade legislators to vote in favor of "my" bills. At one point I was frantically tracking the progress (or lack thereof) of as many as 168 different bills during one legislative session which included reform in the areas of child abuse, neglect, abandonment, support, custody and domestic violence and abortion rights. (This offered me my first exposure to Sarah Palin, the Mat-Su anti-Choice citizen of the 1990s.) I worked tirelessly in order to strengthen laws in Alaska that would protect children.

As unique as Alaska is, we struggled with many of the same issues as all Americans, with some very different ones as well. Because we were so small and so sparsely populated, it did require a special brand of individualism. But there was fairness in the state and though many of its immigrant population came North in search of unequaled (and unrealistic) fortunes, we were not intolerant of all the diverse personalities that laid claim to their little corner of Alaska.

That didn't last and our politics definitely became more conservative. My work was challenging and I told reporters one day that I might feel more productive if I simply came to work and pounded my head against the outside wall of the Capitol and retreated home. We were suddenly saddled with social conservative majorities and it was a nail-biting fight to the end of each session.

What *has* changed in Alaska is the state's population and its politics. It not only became very conservative, Christian conservative mixed with anti-government conservative, but that was all topped off with a whole lot of interest in the wealth that the resources of the State have to offer to corporate developers. It is not the Alaska I grew up in. It really has become *"Palin's Alaska."*

We must stop this accelerated interest in Palin that has turned into this twisted perception that she is somehow a folk-hero for the "common man." We must understand with whom she *really* identifies. We must stop her, and those like her, from further igniting the extremism and risking the spread of the tide of radical religious agendas, and prevent it from bleeding over into our politics in the rest of the country, resulting in a *"Palin's America."*

.

7 A Word About "TheoPalinism"

"Extremism is Dangerous Even When it Wears a Pretty Face"

Right after hearing the announcement that Palin was chosen as the VP nominee I burned up my former laptop in a mad flurry of expression and the result was a rant written in three weeks called *"TheoPalinism: The Face of Failed Extremism."* It was a release of frustration over her appointment to be sure, but it was more than that. I self-published that rant and released it on October 22, 2008 referring to her as "failed" before the first vote was cast. I was willing her to lose in my own determined way.

I called it *"TheoPalinism"* which is a play on words by merging theocracy and Palin. She earned this honor because as a public administrator she made decisions for her "subjects" without their knowledge or consent. She chose to dedicate her town and the whole state of Alaska to the God of her faith, *and yes, she actually formally did that.* I thought it was quite clever when I coined TheoPalinism a couple of years ago but then quickly learned just how many people in this country do not recognize or know the definition of the word "theocracy."

Am I saying we are ignorant? Most of us, no. To me, the fact that this word is foreign to us says that we Americans are damn lucky! And though I have to define that word for us here, I do so because it is the single greatest threat to our democracy. We are now forced to understand its true meaning and the seriousness of what that could do to our existence as we know it.

Why does it matter now? Well, much ado was made about some very real myths, and I hear them repeated to me even now by those who defend her. My response to these myths was to, easily and without effort, punch so many holes in them that she wouldn't be able to bail fast enough to keep from sinking. Whether or not she is *ever* an elected official again, we have to wake up as to why this person was touted as such an example of responsible governance, why she actually had an 80% approval rating when first elected as Governor in Alaska, or how she even won that election. My favorite Palin boast, how *"I took down the good 'ol boy network,"* must be put into perspective.

I know it is unpleasant to have to wade through the low-tide silt and mud of "Palin-land;" I have been doing it for far too long. And some of you just may not be able to stomach it, period. But misery loves company – so join me. TheoPalinism has been republished (and slightly updated) by Lexovien Publishing, the same company which is offering the book you are now reading.

My father even contributed a chapter on Troopergate. This is significant because as Commissioner of Public Safety from 1974-1978 he served in the Cabinet of Governor Jay S. Hammond, and then served again as Commissioner in Governor Walter J. Hickel's Cabinet from 1990-1994. Because of his influence in legislation and writing regulation for that department over the years, there is hardly another more qualified to speak to the ethics violation Palin was found guilty of regarding the firing of her Trooper ex-brother-in-law than my father. You may find it interesting.

Initially, I had thought to include *TheoPalinism* as part of *God, Guns and Greed.* I made the decision not to, as I did not want this book to focus unduly on Palin; the picture here is much bigger. However, if you're interested in exploring this further, TheoPalinism is available on Amazon and elsewhere.

So where does that lead us to from here? - *smack dab into politics!*

8 The "Chosen"

"I like your Christ; I do not like your Christians. Your Christians are so unlike your Christ" ~ Mahatma Gandhi

Also known as the "elect," there is a new name for this philosophy of Christianity in which Palin grew up. It is emerging as the largest Christian non-denomination-denomination in America, yet no one has ever heard of it. It is *Dominionism*. The following is as succinct a definition as I can communicate to describe to you just what Dominionism is. Once you understand what Dominionism is you will be astounded and appalled at how frequently you start seeing elements of it virtually everywhere you look and listen.

Here is that definition:

Dominionism 101

In its simplest form, Dominionism is a political approach to Christian faith and practice based on a literalistic interpretation of Chapter 1 verses 26 - 28 of the Book of Genesis. Dominionists perceive themselves as the 'Chosen' and are commanded to 'subdue' the earth and "have dominion" over all living creatures.

The goal of Dominionism is to abolish the separation of Church and State and to establish the United States as a distinctively Christian nation based upon Old Testament Mosaic Law. Dominionism is an umbrella term that harbors many divergent groups claiming a foundation in Christianity.

You must be 'born again,' must accept Jesus Christ as your Lord and Savior, and must profess a personal relationship with Christ." ~ Leah L Burton

All Christians are <u>not</u> Dominionist - but all Dominionists <u>claim</u> Christianity

A "walkaway" from Dominionism put it this way: *"They use the term 'born again' to differentiate themselves from other Christians. Only the 'born again' go to heaven in their mind."*

A walkaway is a person who does precisely that. They walk away from Dominionism. They are often times full of fear and feel as though they are alone in doing this, not knowing that there are tens if not hundreds of thousands of walkaways worldwide.

Dominionists refer to them as "fallen away" from the church which has a different connotation completely. Walking away takes tremendous strength and courage. The church members admonish them and warn them that they are letting Satan in if they leave. This is why the church calls them "fallen" indicating that they have fallen into Satan's lair.

This person who described the pious sense of superiority of a "born again" is a friend and colleague who walked away from the Assemblies of God, one of many churches that comprise the bible-based cult of Dominionism. She was not just a member of Dominionism for 37 years, she was an ordained minister. One can only imagine the personal struggle that she endured to make that decision.

Understanding Dominionism is crucial before being able to take this discussion on to the next step. In order define it in plain terms, I had to settle on a term that we could all grasp and Dominionism is the one I chose that provided the strongest chance of becoming "branding" for this Movement. After numerous discussions and debates with other researchers across America, I was given a collective nod by those who I respect to take this definition and run with it.

Branding is used in marketing to identify something to make it stand out. For example, we tend to say make a "Xerox" when we want a copy, or grab a "Kleenex" when we want a "tissue." We know that a rainbow colored apple with a bite out of it represents Apple, Inc. the computer company, and after the nightmare disastrous oil spill in the Gulf of Mexico in 2010, most of us now recognize the British Petroleum logo even without the "BP" when we see that kaleidoscope-looking green and yellow sun. This is "branding" and it really is a powerful way to identify a message, product and/or an entity.

Glazing Over and Nodding Off

I don't know about you, but I admit that this is what I did in church for the majority of the hours I sat in those pews as a youth. I kicked my feet while being "Shhhh'd" by my mom and colored the program of the day's hymns and sermon, all the while hearing the Pastor's words as background noise to my daydreams. This is *not* what I want to have happen here with my readers. It is challenging, to say the least, to take such a serious and comprehensive topic and then write about it without losing everyone's interest. I am endeavoring to make this as pleasant a trek as possible as we traverse through a very dark and foreboding world about America's homegrown religious extremism by bringing in the lighter side and the positives of how we are not powerless!

What I do hope you feel is a range of emotion concerning these difficult topics. Anger, indignation, surprise, annoyance, any and all of these will come naturally to you as I give you the "Reader's Digest" version of this movement. Writing this as an overview is essential or I risk having all of you glazing over and nodding off. I get it; it is hard to make this appealing without sounding like a tinfoil-hat conspiracy theorist or a dry and boring lecturer. There isn't a whole lot of "sexy" in this message, that's for sure, but there is a great deal of disconcerting and downright frightening information in this exposé.

It requires repeating that I am the messenger because that is my role in starting this conversation. There are many, many experts who have researched, studied and written about the dangers of Dominionism in America and abroad and I can point you in the direction of their academic and journalistic works so that you can read more if inclined. But suffice it to say that I am here to begin the dialogue. Forget the adage that we are never to discuss politics and religion in polite company. Frankly, that simply isn't working out so well for us right now.

It is inarguably disturbing to read about this at times. It's also unsettling to think that these extreme believers, though a minority, have gained so much influence in our political arena, including the ability to mold our laws. I absolutely understand the desire may be to put this book down and to ignore the idea that Dominionists really are a threat. It is tempting to think that if we ignore them, they just might somehow "go away."

On the other hand, I am confident that once you have sunk your teeth into this, some of you may find yourself yearning to understand even more about this very real and immediate threat. You will genuinely be blown away to learn of the vast number of scholars, theologians, and investigative journalists who have all written in depth about theocracy in America, where religion sets the foundation for the rule of law. You may be shocked to learn that some of these works have been in print for decades and no one has ever heard of them. I will include the names of just some of the authors that I personally highly recommend at the back of this book. It is imperative that we understand as *much* as we can. Knowledge is power and puts *us* in the driver's seat when it comes to shutting this extremism down in America. We *must* grab the wheel; the question is from whom?

The answer is: Political Dominionists.

Identifying Dominionists is Like Playing "Whack-a-Mole"

Taking the wheel away from these Dominionists requires that we identify just whom exactly we are talking about, and that is not always so easy with this crowd. They come in varying shades of revisionist Christianity, and belong to different denominations. In addition, they often don't agree with each other, but they do share a common goal to achieve "dominion" world-wide in the name of Jesus Christ their Lord and Savior. They even have their own versions of the Bible, each claiming emphatically that theirs is the *only* way to the Kingdom of Heaven, eternal salvation, forgiveness and everlasting life – no haughtiness there, eh?

I have had conversations with some purists that suggest it is inaccurate to lump all these "Dominionists" under one term, but I disagree. One of the very reasons that this is not getting out and into the mainstream consciousness of Americans is that the movement is fractured into an unbelievable number of little sub-groups. This is not accidental. In fact, when anyone gets just a little too close for comfort there are those (i.e. the Assemblies of God Churches) who practice what they call "condemnation and rebranding" in order to evade notice and to re-invent their identity. It is very effective and has worked time and time again. We can see it in their religious practices *and* their political agendas.

There are so many segments involved in the study and monitoring of Political Dominionism that a person can literally spend all their time on just one aspect. This umbrella term of Political Dominionism casts its shadow over such a variety of divergent participants that it is virtually impossible to name them all, but for the sake of argument and information here is a rambling list, a *partial* list, of those who you can visualize dangling from individual threads and twisting in the winds of religious extremism under my umbrella of Political Dominionism. A smattering of names and organizations dangling on those strings under the Political Dominionist umbrella for example are:

Calvinists
Third Wave
Pentecostals
Neopentecostals
Religious Right
Christian Reconstructionists
Christian Nationalists
New Apostolic Reformationsists
Fundamentalists
Evangelicals
Pre-tribulational Premillenialism
Post- tribulational Premillenialism
Post-millenialism
Amillenialism

...(deep breath)...Transformation Network; 7 Mountains Mandate; Southern Baptists Convention; Global Harvest Ministries; C. Peter Wagner; R.J. Rushdoony; Gary North; Rick Warren; Rick Joyner; Cindy Jacobs; Dutch Sheets; Os Hillman; ...(by the way I just listed most of who endorsed Governor Rick Perry's tent revival "The Response" that took place in Houston, Texas August 6, 2011 – coincidence? No...)

...(okay...*another* deep breath!) Ted Haggard; D. James Kennedy; Don & Anna Warrick & Cadets for Christ; Christian Embassy; Campus Crusade; Watchman on the Walls; Fellowship of Christian Athletes; Franklin Graham & Samaritan's Purse; Billy Graham; Lou Engle & The Call...(a couple of Palin Pals in that group and above)...

...(one more time! Breathe!)...James Dobson & Focus on the Family; Donald Wildmon, Bryan Fischer & American Family Association; Tony Perkins & The Family Research Council; Ralph Reed; Phyllis Schlafly & Concerned Women for America; Doug Coe & The Family; John Hagee; Dr. Sun Yat-Moon; ...and SO many more it would make its own volume to this book! (Note: I have included the dead and the living in this list.)

As I said, it really is impossible to list them all here, and believe me - my research associate, Alex Bird, and co-author of our next book and I have compiled an impressive list that count into the thousands. We will be diagramming those connections in our next book, *"The Charts: Connecting the DOTS."* Visual presentation is the only way to truly see this dangerous web of extremism in America, as this short list shows us, it can get overwhelming very quickly.

The intentional obscurity of their organizations and the shakers and movers in Dominionism makes them hard to identify. Bruce Wilson, who writes for www.talk2action.org is a dedicated researcher and colleague who said this:

> *"The [Dominionists] "Third Wave" movement is cross-denomination and is not synonymous with any specific denomination, nor is it synonymous with Evangelical or Fundamentalist. Although the movement emerged from Pentecostalism, it draws its support from a variety of denominations and religious streams.* **They believe they are**

> *forming a post-denominational church to take the world for the end times."*

See what I mean? Phew! Even we have a hard time explaining it all to each other. They are "this," they aren't "that," but sometimes they are one or more and occasionally ALL the above!   HUH??? Say what?

Charting their identities and descriptions is really only understandable in a visual format like an "Org Chart" (organizational chart as in a corporate hierarchy). Read what Chris Hedges, author of New York Times bestseller "American Fascists" has to say about this,

> *Dominionism takes its name from Genesis 1:26-31, in which God gives human beings "dominion" over all creation. This movement, small in number but influential, departs from traditional evangelicalism. Dominionists now control at least six national television networks, each reaching tens of millions of homes, and virtually all of the nation's more than 2,000 religious radio stations, as well as denominations such as the Southern Baptist Convention. Dominionism seeks to redefine traditional democratic and Christian terms and concepts to fit an ideology that calls on the radical church to take political power. Dominionism, born out of a theology know as Christian Reconstructionism, seeks to politicize faith.*
>
> *The movement has seized control of the Republican Party. Radical Dominionists have no legitimacy. They are manipulating Christianity (and millions of sincere believers) to build a frightening mass movement.*

Another researcher, Mantis Kantz, makes this excellent observation as she talks about a powerful Dominionist organization in Washington, D.C. that has been made quite public due to the work of Jeff Sharlet in his very successful book in 2009 *"The Family: The Secret Fundamentalism at the Heart of American Power."* Replace "The Family" in her explanation with "Dominionists" and you will see the pattern of unmistakable similarity:

> *Associating these groups (or, for that matter, any organization, church, politician, dictator, CEO, lobbyist or evangelical) with The Family (Dominionists) is, by design, convoluted. The Family (Dominionists) collects no dues, wears no robes, maintains no official membership roster, nor even a website.*
>
> *And while their mission is decidedly ultra-conservative, American and evangelical in nature, those who stand under the umbrella of The Family (Dominionism)come from all religions, faiths, nationalities and political persuasions. Not all who work for The Family (Dominionists) are members, per se, nor have even heard of The Family (Dominionists) or know the nature of its work.*
>
> *As a body, The Family (Dominionism) is amorphous. It is the sum total of all its parts, with each part contributing to the Fellowship's (Dominionists) work – even as they may operate independently of and/or be entirely oblivious to the greater, collective cause they are serving. It is their*

68

contribution to this cause that binds them to the body.

It makes no difference whether their contribution is intentional or incidental, so long as it serves a role in promoting [the Family] [Dominionism]. - Mantis Kantz

See what I mean? This took considerable work on their part to create a movement that could operate in the open yet no one sees them - admittedly very, *very* clever. And they have contingency plans to cover their tracks in the event exposure occurs: Flat out deny! And hey! It is working so far. They can literally be standing there with one hand about to red-pen our U.S. Constitution and ready to sew the Christian cross over the field of stars on the flag, while the other hand is balancing the Bible, and yet no one notices! Even then, caught completely in the act, they will look you straight in the eyes and bold-faced LIE! Insisting that they aren't doing any such thing! To date, we have let them get away with it. And when I say "we," I mean all of us, whether liberal, conservative or apolitical. What they do affects us all whether you choose to ignore them or not.

Then, no sooner does a researcher, such as myself, begin to shine a light on them than they scurry into the darkness only to emerge again with a new identity. This is that process I spoke of earlier, the "condemn and rebrand" sleight-of-hand. When one or more aspect of their activity is revealed, they simply pull out the stationary and write a letter declaring *"Nuh-uh, that wasn't us! We don't even <u>agree</u> with that way of thinking."*

Immediately after Perry's show in Houston, "The Response," Michelle Goldberg wrote an excellent article for The Daily Beast titled, "A Christian Plot for Domination?" that finally got the attention of news shows like Wolf Blitzer's the Situation Room, Jack Cafferty, Rachel Maddow and more. This was an exciting moment for many of us – including the top Dominionists themselves who put our email alerts convincing people that they are not Dominionists. It's that "condemn & rebrand I just spoke of.

Now mind you, the person who invented the New Apostolic Reformation and is at the top of the Dominionist org chart, C. Peter Wagner, who is adamantly back peddling as fast as possible from the term 'dominion' by telling us all that it is not dominion they are after, is still selling his book simply titled, *"Dominion!"* – and the exclamation point is his title. (I can take bets on how fast that book title and cover will change).

Now, before people get all "wee-wee'd up" (as Palin likes to say), and start telling me that I am way off base in lumping this list under one umbrella, I have already acknowledged that many of these people and groups do not necessarily agree with each other at all. Take Jerry Falwell and Pat Robertson as an example. It goes further than that: these partners with a common cause include motivations and philosophies that are completely non-religious as well, such as corporatists and your garden variety anti-government types. They recognize in each other common goals that would benefit and empower all involved, beginning with the act of privatizing government and de-regulating oversight of corporate America. That puts them in the same "bed" when they link arms and agree on a launching point of where they intend to take this country. It is all in their own best interests, but most definitely not OURS!

So for those who tell me they don't "see" any Dominionists in their communities, and tell me, *"This is really scary, good thing there aren't that many of them."* this warning is for you. Look around you. As you learn more you will be amazed at how widespread this is. And THAT is very frightening.

Going Up!

Ergo – the much-needed development of a term to define this movement that I could explain simply in two minutes or less. In corporate America, this is often referred to as one's "elevator speech." Pretend you are on an elevator travelling ten floors with a stranger and you only had that amount of time to describe your message. Until now, the many voices who have written to warn us about this extremism, some with tremendous passion, have simply failed to grab America's attention. Many have tried, but it has been as though they were on an elevator in the tallest building in the world and the elevator was making stops on every single floor. Their audience was getting on and off the elevator at various floors and NO one was listening! Okay, enough said about that. I am sure you get my point.

So what does that mean for the rest of us? It means the majority of us are unaware of Dominionism and therefore we aren't recognizing it when it is right in front of us. So let's talk about all this. All of us, and not just those like me who are already reading/listening/watching politics and issues affecting the separation of church and state. And we need to not only start talking, we need to talk in a way that makes this information accessible. Some of the absolutely best articles and books on this even put *me* to sleep, and I am truly more than mildly interested.

The information is out there. With over 40 books available that have been written since 1988 by people who range from doctoral students, theologians, lawyers, political journalists and those who have "walked away" from Dominionism after having a spiritual epiphany, we have a lot of resources to pull from.

IF we were all getting their message, we would be completely outraged and hollering at the top of our lungs about this push to turn our country on its ear by those that consider themselves "the chosen," these zealots who would make rules we would be controlled by whether we like it or not. We, who are considered by Dominionists to be either "lost" or "damned" and "unchurched," there is not a lot of gray area with them. Trust me, you either convert or are thrown under the bus.

There are a half a dozen researchers on the internet in the area of American religious extremism and its effects both here and abroad who I enjoy working with periodically as an informal collaboration. Their works are extensive and I encourage you to go to their websites (*those too will be listed in the back under references*), and to search the internet for their many articles and read their books to learn tremendous detail on this topic.

Now back to the discussion.

9 The Faces of Political Dominionism

"Perry, Palin, Bachmann...et al"

Sarah Palin wasn't the first Dominionist political candidate, nor will she be the last, but it can be said with certainty that she has become the Poster Gal for this religious political movement. The "new kids" on the block that are emerging are Texas Governor Rick Perry and Minnesota U.S. Representative Michele Bachmann just to name two, and you can bank on the fact that there will be many more in the future. Former Minnesota Governor Tim Pawlenty was another who cast his hat into the 2012 GOP bid for President (but slipped into obscurity before getting started on his campaign.) Nonetheless, he too is a Dominionist conservative who even produced an ad to bolster his conservative Christian bona fides but to no avail. Frankly, he just wasn't Dominionist enough.

That last detail will haunt all other non-Dominionist candidates like the Mitt Romneys and Jon Huntsmans who are Mormons, or the Newt Gingriches and Rick Santorums who are Catholic. Their runs for President will not receive conservative support from this incarnation of the Republican Party until the Party rids itself of these religio-political extremists.

In the meantime, we are going to see a continuing line-up of increasingly more religious conservative candidates offered up as political conservatives. Even now the mainstream media cannot bring themselves to reveal the religious platforms from which these folks are springing. Rather they paint them as a less innocuous threat by calling them "social values" candidates or "social conservatives," or, my favorite, "family values."

One thing is clear: Most Americans have little awareness as to who these people are and what their theological beliefs are. Because they have co-opted Christianity and are quick to invoke God, Jesus Christ and call themselves Christian they are seen as good god-fearing Americans and not members of a dangerous movement to "reclaim America for Christ," disavowing all other faiths. They are hiding this in plain sight, but few of us are paying attention. And that is what they rely on.

If you push back against them, you are labeled as anti-Christian, anti-religion, even anti-American. I know because I get this every day in my work to expose Dominionism in American Politics. In fact, even though I was baptized and raised Lutheran I am told that I am "not the right kind of Christian." Exactly this happened in Sarah Palin's first mayoral election in Wasilla, Alaska. She referred to herself as "Wasilla's first Christian mayor." Her predecessor, a Lutheran, took offense at that and released a list showing the church affiliations of himself, and the previous eight (Christian) mayors.

What complicates getting the message out even more is the fact that most of us have no idea who these "up and comers" in Dominionist politics are. They have little-to-no name recognition and in many ways enjoy hiding behind the constant attention misdirected to Palin (and now to Bachman as well) who attracts it to herself constantly. She is the magnet that keeps people distracted and wondering what *her* next move might be, which is all the better for them in so many ways. It allows them to skirt questions about their religious beliefs. They know it is a benefit to thump the Bible; they just don't want the queries to dig down too deep.

Palin has become, at a minimum, a distraction that diverts our attention away from what is building in the background of conservative politics across America. Whether she is ever an elected official again or not, she continues to suck the air out of someone's room each time she emerges on FOX. Regularly, I will read of people mocking, chuckling and/or not taking her involvement in this dangerous game seriously. I get that. The material that originates from her very own camp and is dropped in our laps does require us to use great restraint *not* to make fun of her on so many levels.

We have to avoid the temptation to treat Sarah Palin as a ridiculous joke. The sad reality in this macabre play is that we must take her seriously. She is a carefully-planned and crafted distraction that keeps us uninformed and our eyes off the ball. That "ball" is the real message of this book: Just who else is in this game? And what exactly IS this game? Why should we take these people seriously? What really motivates them? Who has the power?

For example, while the country is busy snickering at the latest tabloid story concerning the Palins, (ranging from speculations about marital difficulties, her daughter's out-of-wedlock pregnancies, or questioning who the real mother might be of Sarah's son Trig,) how many of us even remotely recognize who the other extremist candidates are who are waiting in the wings? In addition to Perry and Bachmann as I noted above, others that should scare the bejeezus out of us as future candidates are Haley Barbour, Lindsay Graham, Jim DeMint, John Thune, Bob McDonnell, Mike Pence and more.

These are all names of people who hold the very same religious-political views as Sarah Palin and they are *all* contemplating a run for President in 2012 or beyond. Some of them actually have political experience and decent educations. What's more, a few of them for many years have been instrumental in powering the machine that is responsible for serving us *up* a "Sarah Palin" candidate.

Michele Bachmann embodies her own version of extreme politics. She is a career politician who actually believes that the government is the enemy, but she can't seem to quit running for re-election. Now, she has even announced her candidacy for president in 2012 – and yes, I really do mean President of the United States.

She has made some remarkably insane statements and claims that rival Palin's outlandish remarks, fueling the fires of extremism, yet Michele gets a fraction of the press that Palin does. While we are distracted by Palin's unpredictable antics, people like Bachmann are contributing just as dangerously to this growing breeding ground of fear and paranoia.

These distractions are understandable. It is a tendency of human nature – a bit like the morbid fascination I referred to earlier when people not only can't turn their heads when passing a car wreck, they actually slow down. Or why do people sit on hard metal benches for hours at a NASCAR race? We all know it is not the stimulation of seeing cars go in circles that holds the interest; it is the anticipation that eventually there may be a spectacular crash. Watching out for what Palin will do or say next appeals to those same innate reflexes. Call it a train wreck or car wreck, doesn't matter; it's still messy. While we really don't want to hear another syllable or see any more contrived facial expressions from her, we still can't help but peak through our fingers, most of us in profound disbelief.

Don't be fooled by all the noise of the Republican leaders either. They may not be able to decide from one moment to the next how to position themselves when it comes to Palin and others like her, but most are enjoying the diversion that she creates. After all, they can pretend that Palin is really the one who holds all those cockamamie positions, not they, even while they stand in the background mumbling in hidden agreement. This agreement doesn't always make noise; their "silence" can be deafening. For instance, how many Republicans do you remember coming forward to denounce the "curb-stomping" in Kentucky when Rand Paul's campaign worker stepped on the face of a young woman who was peacefully protesting his campaign before the 2010 midterm elections? None? You would be correct. That is what I mean by agreeing without using their voices, by consciously making their decision to do and say nothing.

After the Tucson shooting of Congresswoman Gabby Giffords and nineteen others, another crescendo of deafening compliance occurred. Immediately after this tragedy, several *Republican* politicians from Arizona, no less, expressed their fears and concerns by resigning, stating that after talking it over with family it just wasn't worth the risk of being shot or subjected to violence of any kind.

Such an out-of-control conservative machine has been created that even their own spin doctors, politicians, and members live in fear of it. Their concerns vary from, at a minimum, chastisement, to all-out retribution if they are perceived not to "go along to get along." Their main worries are from those on the far-right fringes, their own supporters that now comprise the Tea Party. A prime example of the growing influence of the Tea Party faction was their grasp on the budget negotiations in Congress that nearly led to America to defaulting on its debt for the first time in U.S. history.

The message has been delivered loud and clear to Democrats and Republicans alike by this haughty crowd who have hit their stride full of puffed up verbosity and a false sense of "self." In fact, after the 2010 midterm elections, Tea Party leaders encouraged activists to "greet" the new Republican members of Congress who they had supported. The message now? *"Warning: We are watching you."*

Now we must do the same. We must watch the Dominionists. And we must watch not only when the noise increases, but when it grows quiet, for when they are the quietest I am the most concerned.

Speaking of "Chosen"

....*Along Comes Queen Esther & The King Davids.*

When Sarah Palin was announced, as I have said, it was so much more than simply her lack of experience that startled me. It was her extreme religious beliefs that I knew from experience were permanently intertwined with her politics, and I wasn't alone. Many who work to preserve the separation of church and state immediately recognized the danger behind this seemingly folksy persona.

Both Queen Esther and King David are characters from the Old Testament. Queen Esther is described as possessing the looks of a beauty queen and a heroine who risked all to "bring her people" to freedom.

"God delivers His people in mysteriously unique ways. The story of Esther demonstrated God's plan of deliverance through the trembling faith of a young Queen's petition. God works within his children preparing them in His time for His tasks. God raised Esther from an orphan to royalty "for such a time as this" (Esther 4:14). Esther fasted, prayed and waited until the time was right to reveal her petition. God delighted to work through her step of faith."

Palin sees herself as the modern day Queen Esther and in fact was anointed as such in her church in Wasilla, Alaska. Palin has stated numerous times that she seeks divine guidance from God in all her decisions. This would not be an issue if it weren't for the fact that Dominionists *believe* that God has mandated them to take dominion over the world.

On his blog at the Wall of Separation, Rob Boston explains that he is not opposed to a candidate who makes references to God. He is opposed to candidates who would let faith do the governing. Referring to a speech

Palin made at her former church in which she stated that the people of Alaska should "get right with God," and that the war in Iraq reflects God's will, Boston chafed at the idea that public officials might hope to mandate the faith of their constituency:

"I don't want the president, governor, or mayor worrying about the state of my soul and whether my neighbors and I are 'right with God.' He or she would do better building the economy, creating jobs and filling potholes. We have great religious freedom in this nation. If any American feels that his or her soul needs a tune-up, there is no shortage of religious leaders willing to help out with that." – Rob Boston AU

Julian Lukins wrote, *"The Faith of Sarah Palin"* in Charisma.[1] This excerpt is important in learning how far back Palin's indoctrination goes"

"SARAH PALIN WAS A LITTLE GIRL HOLDING on to her mom's hand when she first attended Wasilla Assembly of God (AG) Church in her hometown of Wasilla, Alaska. The church's founding pastor, Paul Riley, remembers the pigtailed second-grader—then Sarah Heath—coming with her mom, Sally. They established a pattern of faithful attendance that continued through Sarah's childhood and teenage years.

Every week, Riley recalls, Sarah attended Missionettes, the church's program for girls. During those formative years, Sarah learned about the Pentecostal tradition, the baptism of the Holy Spirit, divine healing and the importance of living out her faith in the world.

By the age of 12, Sarah showed depth in her personal faith, Riley told Charisma.

'She began to have a strong desire for the Lord,' he says.

One summer's day in 1976, 12-year-old Sarah waded into the chilly waters of Beaver Lake, a popular location for church camps. She had committed her life to Jesus and wanted to be baptized along with her mom and sister. Riley immersed Sarah in the lake, baptizing her in the name of the Father, the Son and the Holy Spirit. 'I wish I could remember more about that moment,' reminisces the retired pastor, now 78. 'I know that she loved the Lord with all her heart.'

After her baptism, Sarah continued to attend Wasilla Assembly of God, growing in her faith and singing in the choir, Riley recalls. 'I know that she did receive an experience of the Holy Spirit," he told Charisma, "and that she received a calling on her life.' That spiritual turning point came when Sarah's youth pastor told her: **'You are called by God for a purpose.' Years later, Palin confided that the pastor's words were etched on her mind.**

Prophetic minister Barbara Yoder, senior pastor of Shekinah Christian Church in Ann Arbor, Michigan, says[2]:

"I believe this is a time of incredible breakthrough for women. I am simple enough to believe that we don't know everything about the way God moves and that [Palin] just might be an Esther."

Mark Arnold [republican supporter], a Charismatic pastor in Hamilton, Ohio, would have to agree. In fact, he felt the Holy Spirit,

> *[...] had given him a message for Palin about being an Esther, but he had no idea how he would deliver it. His opportunity came at a McCain-Palin campaign stop in Ohio last September. Incredibly, Arnold found himself just feet away from Palin and McCain at the podium after being asked to escort a group of Boy Scouts to the front—even though he was not a Boy Scout leader.*
>
> *What happened next was remarkable. "[Palin] was on her knees, hugging a lady who had lost her son in Iraq," Arnold told Charisma. "She spun around, looking right at me, and I told her:* **'God wants me to tell you that you are a present-day Esther.' She began to cry and shake my hand in an affirming way. She said, "Yes, I receive that. ... Please keep praying for me,'"** *says 47-year-old Arnold.*[3]

And according to Palin's spiritual advisor, Mary Glazier, it bears repeating here that Glazier told us how,

> *We actually began to pray for [Palin] before she became mayor of Wasilla, Glazier says.* **We felt then that she was the one God had selected.**
>
> *She asked me to pray with her for wisdom and direction," Glazier recalls. 'I sensed a real heart of surrender to the will of God in her. God often chooses the least likely people to be at the forefront, and* **I**

do believe that God has equipped [Palin] for this hour.'

Glazier told all of this to Charisma, a Christian magazine, that members of her organization, Windwalkers, had received words of knowledge about Palin being *"called to impact the nation."* At that point, they had no idea she would be running for the office of vice president of the United States. But remember, she has told us repeatedly that she does have that fire in her belly!

Palin is verifiably a Dominionist. She takes what she believes to the requisite biblically-based position on a variety of political issues. This includes denial of global warming, being anti-abortion, against gay rights, for the privatization of education and pretty much all of government, for pushing revisionist history into public education, and including intelligent design as science. It also means being against any Palestinian state. Love, love, love Israel, but Jews... not so much!

...and... God has called her to serve.

Perry

Governor Rick Perry of Texas is one of our "King Davids" in conservative politics. We have seen others such as former South Carolina Governor Mark Sanford who even referred to himself as King David at a press conference (oddly while trying to explain his tryst to South America to be with his mistress.) Or John Ensign who stalked his mistress and used money and influence to satisfy his lust for her while married and voting in Congress to regulate the morals of others. Both were frat boys at the C Street House that Sharlet writes about in *"The Family"* along with a lengthy list of mostly conservative, but a smattering of blue dog liberals who lived there as well.

Rick Perry is Palin in a guy suit. A Methodist in his early years he now attends Dominionist churches, including openly associating with one of the most powerful Dominionist churches in America, Cornerstone, headed by controversial Dominionist preacher John Hagee.

Perry unabashedly promoted a modern day tent revival named, "The Response" that was billed as an "apolitical religious gathering."4 That could not have been further from the truth. This was about nothing BUT politics and religion! The truth, however, rarely gets in the way of their actions. In fact, with the help of the entertainers at FOX these candidates and politicos have a 24/7 open mike to convey their rhetoric and the FOX employees, who are never stumped by truth, and who enthusiastically promote them.

America is just "meeting" Perry and most have welcomed him as a good Christian man, like George W. for whom he worked and with whom he attends church with on occasion. The event that Perry orchestrated with the help and endorsement of numerous Dominionist leaders such as C. Peter Wagner, David Barton, John Hagee, James Dobson, Tony Perkins, Bryan Fischer, C.L. Jackson, Cindy Jacobs, Mike Bickle, and a much longer list of names attracted a fair following on a hot summer day in Houston, Texas.

Many of us who follow this Bible-based cult were also tuned in to the show to monitor what was going on behind what mainstream media would glean from it. Here is the post I did for my web site God's Own Party." com the following day.

My "Response" to Perry's Altar Cult

Yesterday, for six and a half hours, I subjected not only myself to the entire broadcast of Texas Governor Rick Perry's "The Response" tent revival in Houston, Texas - but my entire household, including pets. All parties looked at me pleading with their eyes that I move on to something different. I am sure a neighbor or two may have benefited from the broadcast as well. It was quite a show.

A friend and fellow researcher was actually at The Response in person, Dr. Anthea Butler of the University of Pennsylvania, professor of theology, along with Sarah Posner - both of whom write for Religion Dispatches. Dr. Butler actually received her doctorate from studies - unlike the parade of "Dr.'s" that graced that stage and endorsed this event. (EVERY one and his brother is an honorary "Dr." in the world of Dominionist entertainment).

As I watched it live on God TV (and yes that really IS the name of the station) I live tweeted with Dr. Butler as she watched it in person. Made for a very interesting perspective on what was transpiring. I will share the highlights from our observations.

Much has been written about it today, but what I am not seeing are reports about some of the more subtle details that took place, rather the focus is on how few people actually attended the event. Today's estimates put the numbers around 22,000 people. Yes, the stadium holds 70,000+, but the fact that they had over 20,000 in attendance is not a huge comfort to me or my fellow researchers.

You see, these attendees are devout! Kool-Aid drinking devout. Every single one of them will cast their vote in 2012 and you can bet it will be for a Dominionist candidate. Not one of these folks will vote for a Mormon or a Catholic, even those who are running as Republicans. It just won't happen. So that leaves an uncertain Perry, Palin, Bachmann field to choose from.

Why does this scare the hell out of me? Well, so many reasons really - not the least of which is the growing absurdity coming from the fringe Left trying to get support for their idea to run a Primary candidate against President Obama. As I just said, these zealots vote. Progressives - better at pontificating than voting. So as it stands, a second term for Obama is threatened already and the last thing we need are Civics-101-challenged disgruntled "lefties" trying to fracture a voter bloc that already can't find the motivation to vote most of the time.

Here are some of the notable moments in Perry's Altar Cult yesterday:

From the first utterance we were off in a Dominionist world of sounding the Shofars and calling all good Christians to action in a prayer and fast sort of way (there were food vendors there). The first to speak was Dr. James Dobson, former head of Focus on the Family before it ran amok financially - dwindling into a nearly non-existent entity - where once it reigned in this world. Then his wife Shirley, the Chair of the National Day of Prayer...well, she prayed of course. And the show was off and running!

They repeatedly laid out the 7 Mountains Mandate to "reclaim" - Family - Religion - Education - Government/Military - Arts & Entertainment/Sports - Media - (and their favorite lately) Education. The 7 Mountain agenda was repeated by the majority of their performers including Perry himself.

They voiced their alliance with Messianic Jews, those that accept Jesus Christ as their Messiah. If the others don't convert they will face the same fate as the rest of us who do not share the Dominionist theology. As I said in one tweet when John Hagee was speaking, a known anti-Semite and faux preacher from Cornerstone Church in San Antonio, Texas that is heavily influential in the Republican Party: "They love, love LOVE Israel! Jews - not so much...."

We witnessed Perry's Anointing! Yep they actually anointed their King David right there on the stage for the world to see. Sarah Palin went through this at her church years ago (As Queen Esther, though - not King David). As the emcee of the moment called for all in attendance to

85

embrace their nearest pastor/preacher/leader, Perry returned to the stage and was embraced by top gun clergy as they called for a "Fresh Anointing."

In addition to repeating the 7 Mountains goals of capturing and dominating those 7 secular areas of culture, they repeatedly referred to themselves as King Davids. King Solomons and Queen Esthers. Their references are not casual, but speak to the mindset that these Dominionist leaders have wherein rules apply to everyone else - just not to them. Take C Street for example, and notice that Sam Brownback was there in person - a regular ol' C Street frat boy in the flesh.

This is significant. It goes hand-in-hand with their belief that they are "The Chosen" - "The Elect." God has spoken directly to them (they claim) to lead their people out of the abyss of immorality and to "reclaim" America for the one true God. This of course is the whole "we were founded as a Christian Nation claim that they spew to all their Sheeples. They clearly know what is best for ALL of us! Just ask them!

They proudly stood in company with political strategists such as Tony Perkins, President of the Family Research Council, while claiming that this was an "apolitical event." The entire Show contained non-stop political rhetoric! But as Professor Butler pointed out, they do not have a care in the world about violating the separation of church and state laws as long as the courts are controlled by Dominionists.

They referred to the Great Commission in which God has commanded them to go and make converts of all peoples and nations. Their version of proselytizing is extreme and aggressive, we are seeing their methods as they use 3rd world countries as their own Petri dishes to test their plans.

Codespeak! The day was riddled with it. Here are just some of the items they repeated:

Outpouring, Spiritual Mapping, Market Place ministries, Authority, beloved, Awakening, 3rd Wave, the mantle, transform, after your hearts, intercession, anointing, "fall away" - just to name a few. Where are we hearing this talk? Sarah Palin and Michele Bachmann use them frequently

Of course, no event like this would be complete without the performances of Lou Engle's entertainers from his travelling Road Show titled, "The Call." (By the way, Palin spoke to Engle just before making her national debut on stage at the GOP Convention in 2008 by cell phone...just sayin'). Their focus is on abortion and they wail and cry out, tears rolling down their cheeks, as they point to this as evidence that America has gone to the Dark Side. (You could see them actually working themselves up emotionally waiting for their turn to take the mic.)

And yes, there was the requisite non-stop Christian rock music playing at varying decibel levels for the entire time. Most "songs" contained 6 to 8 (and often times 7) words that were repeated over and over and over and over....with a purposeful hypnotic rhythm playing that never stopped. This background of music and repeated refrains that ebbed and flowed throughout the entire performance was orchestrated and intentional - just like everything else they produce.

For those who actually watched any of this yesterday, what is important to understand is that this is their gig. They perform at events like this weekly and sometimes more often than that. Their crowds swell to 100,000 in some parts of the world and the United States. Hell, even their mega-church congregations range in the 10 - 20,000 range on a weekly basis! So while some are minimizing the numbers who attended "The Response" - let's not get cocky.

The rocking, the waving of hands in the air, the outstretched palms are a trademark behavior of these audiences. (I have to tell you that a chill ran through me watching thousands in a trance with outstretched right arms in a salute that was all too reminiscent of the Nazi salute.) They are lured and lulled into this very hypnotically. Fear of damnation and lost salvation consume them mixed with an inflated sense of superior exceptionalism as "true" followers and believers in Jesus Christ. And that means apart from all of us who are "not the right kind of Christian" (meaning we can't produce a born again birth certificate attesting to our status as one of the "saved").

Those of us who research and follow this know that there are approximately 80 million followers in our country alone. Dominionists proudly tout that the number is 104 million. And not to beat a dead horse - but I have to repeat - THEY VOTE!

Oh! And before I forget, we will await the announcement that this anointed King David will be running for president of the United States...any moment now. **Let the battle of "The Chosen" begin!**

Perry is verifiably a Dominionist. He takes what he believes to the requisite biblically-based position on a variety of political issues. This includes denial of global warming, being anti-abortion, against gay rights, for the privatization of education and pretty much all of government, for pushing revisionist history into public education, and including intelligent design as science. It also means being against any Palestinian state. Love, love, love Israel, but Jews... not so much!

...and... God has called him to serve.

Bachmann

Minnesota U.S. House of Representative Michele Bachmann is a born again graduate of Oral Roberts University (how Dominionist is that?!)

Ms. Bachman has some very radical ideas and beliefs about many "button" issues. This includes regarding the U.S. Census as some sort of plot, or believing that President Obama was not born in the United States and is a socialist. In fact, she has such dramatically differing views from most Republicans that she pushed several influential ones to vote for Obama in 2008. She is embraced by the most entrenched extremists in the Tea Party, and on top of all that, need I mention that she is absolutely ill-equipped to lead this country. Democrats and Republicans alike agree with that. Her support is coming purely from the fringe of both the Tea Party and uber-conservative Christians, most of whom have never heard the term Dominionist.

Their own words are always the best way to convey their message so he is an excerpt from an article about Bachmann by Christine Roberts of the New York Daily News wrote:

The Minnesota congresswoman said **she received a "calling" to enter the 2012 presidential race**. She spoke in an interview with Iowa Public Television on Friday.

"Well, every decision that I make, I pray about, as does my husband, and I can tell you, yes, **I've had that calling and that tugging on my heart that this is the right thing to do**," Bachmann said.

Bachmann says she experienced a similar type of spiritual guidance in 2006 when she ran for Congress from Minnesota.

"God then called me to run for the United States Congress. And I thought, what in the world would that be for? And my husband said, "You need to do this," Bachmann said at The Living Word Christian Center, a megachurch in Minnesota, during her campaign.

Bachman is verifiably a Dominionist. She takes what she believes to the requisite biblically-based position on a variety of political issues. This includes denial of global warming, being anti-abortion, against gay rights, for the privatization of education and pretty much all of government, for pushing revisionist history into public education, and including intelligent design as science. It also means being against any Palestinian state. Love, love, love Israel, but Jews... not so much!

...and... God has called her to serve.

Bush

"Is our children learning? Childrens do learn" ~ GWB, Jr.

Now, before you shake your head and say, "Wait a minute! What about Bush?" Well, what *about* Bush? Yes, he is indeed a Dominionist as well, just not the sharpest tool in the shed. Besides that, no one anointed him.

But here is the *bigger* lesson for all those who argue relevance with me about the growing cast of zealots, including the ones I just listed – he was our last President! This is why I find myself dumbfounded by our short-term memory when warning about the very real danger of a Perry, Palin, Bachmann & Co. candidate actually winning! We were just there. What is there not to get about this?

Just look at the references he made about his Mission to Iraq being a "Holy War." Andrew Brown reported this on the web site the guardian.co.uk:

> *In the winter of 2003, when George Bush and Tony Blair were frantically gathering support for their planned invasion, Professor Thomas Römer, an Old Testament expert at the University of Lausanne, was rung up by the Protestant Federation of France. They asked him to supply them with a summary of the legends surrounding Gog and Magog and as the conversation progressed, he realized that this had originally come, from the highest reaches of the French government.*

President Jacques Chirac wanted to know what the hell President Bush had been on about in their last conversation. Bush had then said that when he looked at the Middle East, he saw "Gog and Magog at work" and the biblical prophecies unfolding. But who the hell were Gog and Magog? Neither Chirac nor his office had any idea. But they knew Bush was an evangelical Christian, so they asked the French Federation of Protestants, who in turn asked Professor Römer.

He explained that Gog and Magog were, to use theological jargon, crazy talk. They appear twice in the Old Testament, once as a name, and once in a truly strange prophecy in the book of Ezekiel [...]"

"And the word of the LORD came unto me, saying, Son of man, set thy face against Gog, the land of Magog, the chief prince of Meshech and Tubal, and prophesy against him, And say, Thus saith the Lord GOD; Behold, I am against thee, O Gog, the chief prince of Meshech and Tubal: And I will turn thee back, and put hooks into thy jaws, and I will bring thee forth, and all thine army, horses and horsemen, all of them clothed with all sorts of armour, even a great company with bucklers and shields, all of them handling swords: Persia, Ethiopia, and Libya with them; all of them with shield and helmet [...]"[5]

In the 1980s Ronald Reagan's Gog was Russia. (Interesting how these inerrant Biblical prophesies and signs can take on such fluidity when it doesn't pan out.) So when George W. Bush was president, while all of the rest of us thought we were fighting for peace (or even oil) in the Middle East, the frightening reality was that the President saw something quit different. His motivation was in his conversation with French President Chirac. He was telling others that this war was about fulfilling Biblical prophecy and the End Times.

Beliefnet.com wrote a post explaining it thusly,

In Genesis and Ezekiel Gog and Magog are forces of the Apocalypse who are prophesied to come out of the north and destroy Israel unless stopped. The Book of Revelation took up the Old Testament prophesy:

'And when the thousand years are expired, Satan shall be loosed out of his prison, And shall go out to deceive the nations which are in the four quarters of the earth, Gog and Magog, to gather them together to battle and fire came down from God out of heaven, and devoured them.'

Bush believed the time had now come for that battle, telling Chirac:

'This confrontation is willed by God, who wants to use this conflict to erase his people's enemies before a New Age begins.'

The story of the conversation emerged only because the Elyse Palace, baffled by Bush's words, sought advice from Thomas Romer, a professor of theology at the University of Lausanne. Four years later, Romer gave an account in the September

2007 issue of the university's review, Allez savoir. The article apparently went unnoticed, although it was referred to in a French newspaper.
  - Beliefnet

Again, this makes a huge point about extremism going unnoticed. Here are just a few random quotes by then President of the United States, Leader of the Free World, George W. Bush.:

Tyrants and dictators will accept no other gods before them. They require disobedience to the First Commandment. They seek absolute control and are threatened by faith in God. They fear only the power they cannot possess -- the power of truth. So they resent the living example of the devout, especially the devotion of a unique people chosen by God.

This crusade, this war on terrorism is going to take a while.

God told me to strike at al Qaida and I struck them, and then he instructed me to strike at Saddam, which I did, and now I am determined to solve the problem in the Middle East.

- George W. Bush, blaming the Holocaust on godlessness, rather than on Christian anti-Semitism of Martin Luther, ignoring the fact that Adolf Hitler repeatedly called himself a Christian, pretended to be obeying Christ. April 19, 2001

He also pulled the same arrogant religious position as Palin did when she first took office as Mayor and then as Governor by dedicating the country to Jesus Christ.

The very first act of the new Bush administration was to have a Protestant

93

Evangelist minister officially dedicate the inauguration to Jesus Christ, whom he declared to be 'our savior.' Invoking 'the Father, the Son, the Lord Jesus Christ' and 'the Holy Spirit,' Billy Graham's son, the man selected by President George W Bush to bless his presidency, excluded the tens of millions of Americans who are Muslims, Jews, Buddhists, Shintoists, Unitarians, agnostics, and atheists from his blessing by his particularistic and parochial language.

*The plain message conveyed by the new administration is that **George W Bush's America is a Christian nation and that non-Christians are welcome into the tent so long as they agree to accept their status as a tolerated minority rather than as fully equal citizens.** In effect, Bush is saying: **'This is our home, and in our home we pray to Jesus as our savior. If you want to be a guest in our home, you must accept the way we pray.** - Alan M. Dershowitz, in "Bush Starts Off by Defying the Constitution," Los Angeles Times, January 24, 2001*

This very same statement was re-asserted by Bryan Fischer, head of the American Family Association (a listed hate group by the Southern Poverty Law Center) in the summer of 2011 when he said the following about religious freedoms in America. (And remember when you read this, that most of these folks believe that the only "real" Christian is their kind of Christian.)

"American Family Association's Bryan Fischer: Religious freedom guaranteed for Christians only"

In the wow, just wow category, Bryan Fischer continued his supremacist ways by stating that constitutional guarantees of freedom of religion applies only to Christians. To wit:

"Islam has no fundamental First Amendment claims, for the simple reason that it was not written to protect the religion of Islam. Islam is entitled only to the religious liberty we extend to it out of courtesy. While there certainly ought to be a presumption of religious liberty for non-Christian religious traditions in America, the Founders were not writing a suicide pact when they wrote the First Amendment." – Bryan Fischer, AFA

As ill-equipped as Bush was to be our president, his religious zealousness was tempered (believe it or not) only by the personal agenda and oil interests of his advisors, his vice-president and his own family. Perry, Palin, Bachmann & CO. will not be so conflicted in their loyalties. They have guzzled the kool-aide and their devotion supersedes the best interests of the American people, all in the name of Allah – OOPS! Sorry...I mean God!

...and

Bush is verifiably a Dominionist. He takes what he believes to the requisite biblically-based position on a variety of political issues. This includes denial of global warming, being anti-abortion, against gay rights, for the privatization of education and pretty much all of government, for pushing revisionist history into public education, and including intelligent design as science. It also means being against any Palestinian state. Love,

love, love Israel, but Jews... not so much! ...and... God has called him to serve.

God Needs to Quit "Calling" these People!

Are you beginning to see a pattern emerge here? Each one of them, as well as others like Tim Pawlenty, and every one of the Congressional members that attend prayer meetings in Room #219[6] in the U.S. Capitol, all feel that God has "called" them into service. Their Facebook page states that they have 369 members in the Congressional Prayer Caucus.

It is so pervasive that I am always astonished when people tell me that I am making this stuff up, or exaggerating the size and importance of it. Maybe it's because I know that this cult exists that it is so abundantly clear to me. They might not have yet taken over the United States, but make no mistake. They have succeeded in a primary goal, which was spelled out in the 1980s when they strategized to take control of the Republican Party.

They began pressuring candidates to pass a litmus test that would reveal whether or not they were Christian enough to run as an "R." They formulated strategy starting at the grass roots levels, targeting school boards, city councils, county seats, state legislatures, judicial appointments, then moving up to Congress and the White House. They loudly and openly proclaimed that it didn't matter what Party you ran in as long as you won! And by God – they are doing a bang up job of getting there!

If all of this is not enough, let me add just one more thing. Numerous leaders of this Dominionist Movement including their Senior Apostles and other self-appointed divine leaders, by way of their own testimonials, state that they routinely hang with J.C. I am not making that up! They proudly talk about a period where several of them had lunch with the big guy, "just hangin'," in Colorado Springs, Colorado. Honestly! And these same folks endorsed and attended Rick Perry's *"The Response."* Additionally, they have direct voice access to Perry, Palin, Bachmann & Co.

OUCH!

They Have Been at this for Decades

We saw the success of the Religious Right's effort in the election of Ronald Reagan. When Pat Robertson, a fellow Dominionist whose lunacy approximates that of Palin's, ran for president, ran for president in both 1992 and 1996 he was buried in failure both times. Unfortunately, I doubt Robertson's loss had anything to do with his Dominionist agenda. He is even quoted as saying very clearly without a shred of equivocation in 1984, *"Our aim is to gain dominion over society."*

Nevertheless, he was forced to concede in the primaries after receiving only 5.02% of the vote amounting to 1,097,446 out of a possible 12 million votes cast despite his high public profile. Even though he had high recognition factor in his favor as the host of the 700 Club, he clearly did not have the "charisma" they attributed to Reagan and now attribute to Palin (as unbelievable as that is to me), and this, not his agenda, contributed to his loss.

Because the Dominionists have been organizing over the last 30-40 years in America this has all led up to 2008 when they made their highest ascent by getting a candidate on the Presidential-Vice Presidential ticket with a frightening potential for success - in making their bid for the White House.

Scripture Twisting & Global Warming – "Drill, Baby, Drill!"

Leah L. Burton

They believe in many self-benefitting renditions of twisted scripture that they have crafted carefully from the Christian faith. It really is actually called, "scripture-twisting." More money means that God truly has chosen you. To heck with the folks that can barely afford to make their mortgage payment but scrape up $500 to hear Palin speak (after all she is divinely blessed). Who cares about those who send their last $25 to the rolling 800 number at the bottom of their television screens because after all, they are told the more they send, the greater their chance of salvation? Apparently this twisted version of Christianity has God keeping track of your deposits. Who knew?

And all that hoopla made over Global Warming! Perry, Palin, Bachmann & Co. categorize this as those darn progressives just getting themselves all wound tight. After all, doesn't everyone understand that God provided us with precisely the amount of resources needed to carry us right up until the End Times? They aren't worried. Depleting resources is a sign that they *embrace*, just like disasters such as earthquakes, typhoons, tsunamis, and out-of-control forest fires. It all fits for them because they believe in the retributive, punishing and warring version of God from the Old Testament. These disasters are clearly just God's way of taking out His anger on innocent lives to demonstrate His power and indicate that Armageddon can be penciled in on our calendars.

The importance of this exists because they really, truly believe this stuff. And if the signs aren't there, by golly, they are going to find them. It all becomes self-fulfilling prophecy, and that becomes exceedingly dangerous for the entire world population. Somehow they have overlooked that God's message was *"Watch therefore, for ye know neither the day nor the hour wherein the Son of man cometh." Matthew 25:13 KJV.*

Instead, these folks are working, fast and furiously, to bring on the Second Coming of Jesus Christ. If that

98

means using up our resources, poking a sharp stick in the sides of Russia, China, North Korea and Iran, so be it, because they "fear not." They themselves are saved and immune. They've seen the Left Behind movie and know that *they* will be the naked bodies sucked into space. So for them, it means nothing to provoke the Second Coming by starting an all out World War III that no one will survive. They truly believe this and are dead serious!

Therefore, even if you think that politics is "just really not for you," we must pay attention to these people. This isn't something that *might* happen; they are already well-entrenched in our government. The infestation of the Republican Party was just one sector that they successfully "took dominion" over, and now we must prevent them from spreading like a cancer.

We are a broad audience; 62% or more of us in America, who are *not* hanging out on the fringes, left *or* right. We actually make up who America *really* is. Now we must take interest and understand what is really afoot.

10 ReBiblican Politics

"Go back to what our founders and our founding documents meant - they're quite clear - that we would create law based on the God of the Bible and the Ten Commandments."
~ Sarah Palin May 6th, 2010

There is hardly any one more supportive of *real* Republicans than I! I would love for them to take their Party back, and this needs to be done quickly before it is destroyed and sent the way of the Whig Party.

Please understand that I have just as difficult a time referring to this new crop of religious-politicians as "Republican," as I have calling Dominionists "Christians." All of you that are *true* Republicans, do not take offense to the title of "ReBiblican Politics," because that is *not* you. They know full well who I am really talking about.

Separation of Church & State

Political Dominionism is a Bible-based sect of Christianity that does not represent mainstream Christians in America, or elsewhere in the world. This is a very powerful, very well-organized and very wealthy religious-political machine that has been driving toward the goal of marrying church and state in America for decades.

For as long as humans have existed there have been politics. And even before the birth of Christianity, beliefs, superstitions and faith have wound their way into the rules that govern peoples. Wars have been fought and massive numbers of lives have been lost in the name of religion. A constant struggle to control land and populations has dictated the formations of rules and laws around the world from the very beginning, so when we see this same struggle for power continuing right before us within our own system of government I am stymied as to why this is such an unbelievable concept for us to take seriously. The refrain "history repeats itself" is not an empty one; rather it is a warning that we must heed.

As society has evolved so have the sophisticated intentions and goals of those who dedicate themselves to obtaining more power and more control. It does not matter whether others agree with them or not, this is about dominion. Religious zealots are undoubtedly a persistent part of this group, but they are certainly not doing this solo. What is making this eternal battle ever more dangerous is the blending of common purposes by other groups who share specific end goals. The common goals are smaller government, privatization, less regulation, a conservative Supreme Court.

Who can argue with smaller government per se? However, Dominionists advocate this to achieve the ultimate goals: implementing favorable legal status for private corporations, and passing conservative religious social laws.

Get Your OWN Party!

This has made strange bedfellows out of some seemingly unusual alliances as I enumerated above. As a result of this coalescing of interests we are losing what *were* the two major political parties in America, the Democratic and Republican Parties. Special interests and corporate coffers have so completely invaded this system that it has become about extreme perspectives more than ever. Over the years we have seen the formation of fledgling political parties which have attempted to rise up and compete with the Democrats and the Republicans, all to no avail. All that resulted each time was a splintering off of voters from these two mainstays and the effect has actually caused unintended damage in the wrong direction.

We have but to look at the candidacy of Ralph Nader in 2000 when he ran for president as the Green Party candidate and the effect that Nader's run had on the presidential race that year. Those most likely to vote Green Party would have voted Democrat, had Green not been an option. The votes that Nader won ultimately cost Gore the Presidency. Thus, the struggle to create a third and subsequent political parties is not only challenging but risky. Unless new parties arise simultaneously on both the right and the left we will see a strengthening of whichever side is rallied around one of the two major parties in place today. Introducing alternatives means that a fracturing of the voter-base is inevitable as we saw in 2000 on the liberal side with Nader and Gore.

Same but Different

Today we are witnessing what at first glance seems like a splintering of the republican voter-base with the formation of the Tea Party in May of 2009. But is it? While some on the left see this as a potential for the splintering effect similar to what happened to the liberals in 2000, overconfidence could backfire. We have but to look at the midterm elections of 2010 to see that though the newly formed Tea Party appeared to spawn its own candidates, they all ran with an "R" by their names as Republican candidates. Conservative voters really maintained their voter bloc.

Instead of splitting the votes and weakening their electoral influence, it is a clever consolidation of numerous diverse factions who will overlook many aspects of its potential leaders as long as they are all playing from the same sheet of music on certain bedrock issues. This is why I came up with the title, *"God, Guns & Greed."* Those are synonymous with Dominionists, Constitutionalists/Secessionists & Corporatists. They have become convinced that no matter how many differences may exist between them, their commonalities are worthy of joining forces. This makes for a tremendously dangerous political concoction, not only for Americans, but for the world-at-large.

United, they make their goals abundantly clear for all to see. All we have to do is open our eyes.

From the beginning of this effort by Dominionists, it became clear that of the two main parties, the Republican Party would be the obvious choice. Using *first* conservative jargon on fiscal issues, and then taking the conversation into social issues territory, it didn't take long to stake a claim on the GOP (Grand Ol' Party). Before long, people who had aligned themselves with politically secular conservatism and took pride in belonging to the Republican Party found themselves being sucked into a religio-political world as the Party's Platform changed to include a conservative Christian agenda.

State Republican Party Preambles began to take on Judeo-Christian language and references to biblical law as we see in today's Texas Republican Party Platform. Here is an introduction by www.theocracywatch.org as they take a portion of this screed and explain its roots in Dominionism:

> *The Texas Republican Party Platform can be read as a blueprint for Bush administration policies, and reflects the values of Dominion Theology.*
>
> *Dominionists believe the federal government should recede into the background. This would be achieved through massive tax cuts. Then the Church would assume responsibility for welfare and education. Tax cuts, Faith-based initiatives and school vouchers are the cornerstone of Bush administration*

domestic policies and recommended in the Texas GOP Platform. These policies are putting the U.S. on the path toward becoming what the Platform calls a "Christian" nation.

Theocracy Watch is one of those excellent resources that I referred to earlier and will be included in the reference list of web sites to visit as you delve deeper into understanding this whole discussion.

This assessment illustrates the merging of their specific religious views into the GOP political machine. I am neither anti-conservative nor anti-Republican. In fact, my father is a Republican. But these zealots even chased him out of his own party with their insistence to incorporate religion into the Party's Platform.

My father was an active member of the Alaska Republican Party. He finally walked out of a state convention and renounced his membership telling them that until they removed religion from the Platform he would no longer participate, and this is a man with devout conservative views in his private life about issues such as abortion. I respect him because he at least recognizes that those personal religious views should not be legislated and do not have a place in politics.

He is not alone. These old guard "Rs" are what I often refer to as "Secular Republicans" or "Eisenhower Republicans." They are now growing the ranks of those voters re-registering as Independents. The extremism has pulled the new incarnation of Republicans who still belong to the Party so far to the right that it has absolutely become the ReBiblican Party. I do not say this in sarcasm – this is fact.

My father and those like him still call themselves Republicans and they are. The Dominionists have co-opted their Party just like they co-opted Christianity. They have redefined words such as patriotism, conservative, progressive and socialism along the way, dramatically changing conservative politics in America today. Their extremism is profoundly... *un*-American.

"What Would Jesus Do?"

I am thinking that they need to quit asking that question. This quote is one that the Dominionists proudly sport on bracelets, hats, shirts and the back of their vehicles to be sure that their sense of pious superiority is up front and center for all of us non-saved people can see. This is another one of those messages that they seem to have not gotten from the Bible. That message about being humble like, Luke 18:14, *"[...] For the proud shall be humbled and the humble shall be honored."* I am not seeing a whole lot of humbling going on in Dominionist circles. In fact, conversely, it is rife with haughtiness. Proverbs 16:18, *"Pride goes before destruction and haughtiness before the fall."* Now *that* is a warning I would pay attention to if I were *these* people.

After all, we are told repeatedly in emphatic declarations by these devout believers that the Bible is the "inerrant' (without error) divinely inspired (from God's lips to the bible-writers ears) literal Word of God, and yet this direct dictation of Jesus Christ and the Lord God Almighty seems to face constant editing. Why, it was just 2010 that a new and improved version of the Bible was released with all the latest updates. It seems to go unnoticed that the Bible is a collection of books that have been translated, written and re-written countless times throughout their existence beginning circa 50-70 A.D. yet they promote as though every word is written in stone.

For a book that they insist contains no errors, the need for ongoing editing sends a confusing message to the rest of us, including mainstream Christians who have been encouraged to both accept Christ *and* keep our critical thinking caps intact.

If they accept every word and punctuation as the "error-free" word of God, why would there even be a need to make corrections or to re-write it? I would think that their argument would be that God would have gotten the message right the first time. It has been shown that the contents of the Bible were voted on and put together by a committee vote in Rome. The New Testament was chosen from a pile of books authored mainly by unknown Greek authors, none of whom actually met Jesus. With the exception of the letters of Paul, the earliest of these writings is presumed to have been approximately 50 years *after* Christ's death. But how many people really notice those tiny re-writes anyway? There I go again... just trying to start trouble with those pesky realities.

But they can't have it both ways (or I should say they shouldn't) but they are clearly getting away with it. It is apparent that when the message needs a little massaging to work to their advantage, then presto! A "clarification" is in order! Seems a bit like dangerous territory, this isn't like playing store as a kid where you get to make up your own rules.

America is a Christian Nation ~ Because Americans are Christians

This is one of those arguments, circular in nature that is easy for the Dominionists and their cohorts to sell, yet is so completely un-American. I know... go figure! After all, their audience is almost exclusively those who pride themselves in being the *true* American – god-fearin', patriotic, blue-blood, gun-totin', family values ladened middle-America! How can they be so far off base on this one? They have been told this repeatedly on a 24/7 infusion of false revisionist American history by a panel of people who profit mightily from their ignorance.

After what we just discussed in regard to their ability to take the Bible and twist the scriptures, is it any surprise that they easily take on the task of doing the very same thing to our founding documents? No. Not at all.

Research numbers show that nearly 70% of Americans self-identify as Christian, it's true. But over

50% of those have not sat on a wooden pew unless it was for the nostalgic annual candlelight Christmas service, a wedding or two, or Grandad's funeral. They haven't touched a Bible unless it had Gideon written on it and they moved it out of the way in need of drawer space at a hotel. What's my point?

My point is that we cannot declare that a simple majority in any way, shape or form, real or convenient, takes precedence over our U.S. Constitution. This very same document, which by the way, goes to great lengths to protect American freedoms, the freedoms of *all* Americans, whether in a majority or minority. I know this may surprise some folks, but we really aren't strictly a democracy where majority/mob rules. It was recognized that the better solution was a democratic republic where a minority's rights cannot be trampled just because they may be different in one way or another. To do so leads directly to oppression.

Christian = Conservative, right?

NO! And this is part of the problem: labeling. There are confusing perceptions bandied about out there for Christians in America, not the least of which is that if you are Christian you must belong to the Republican Party. You can't possibly be liberal/progressive (or otherwise) and call yourself a Christian. This is pure nonsense that is being doled out, and believed, by too many Americans.

Fortunately, we have more and more mainstream Christians who notice these inconsistencies and are becoming concerned about the changes happening within their own congregations. They have begun asking questions about the changes that are redefining Christianity in America and showing up in their very congregations through subtle and insidious teachings, such as the notion that all Liberals are secular Atheists, or that as good Christian conservatives their vote must match the "Voter Guide" received in church to avoid eternal damnation. (This was actually stated openly by leading preachers: "Vote Obama/[and you] Go to hell").[7]

In fact, even within Dominionist congregations it is safe to say that many of the individuals who work for and/or attend services numbering into the millions in America alone, are completely unfamiliar with the details of Dominionism. They have little to no understanding that their religious beliefs have been molded and are being reshaped right before their eyes. If asked, most would tell you they have never heard of "Dominionism." Their actions, in their view, are simply being encouraged in the name of what they have been taught is Christianity.

This is one of the many frustrating components of this battle against extremism. Many of their adherents have been lured into this movement on a handful of selling points. They use political and emotional hot-buttons that keep the congregations motivated and focused such as abortion and gay rights, which always rank in the top two positions. There are several more that change from time to time but often include topics such as stem cell research, education and Christian nationalism and more recently secular humanism.

All of this occurs without these folks even recognizing that the Christianity they once knew has transformed through a process called "steeplejacking."

Steeplejacking America's mainstream Christians

This is a very real practice that has turned mainstream Christianity into a shell of what it once was. Traditional churches have had to close their doors in response to the siphoning off of their congregants, leaving their pews empty. Two pastors from the United Church of Christ collaborated and wrote a book on this very subject. Sheldon Culver, an ordained minister for over thirty years, serves on the conference staff of the Missouri Mid-South Conference of the United Church of Christ. Rev. Dr. John Dorhauer is a member of the conference staff for the Missouri Mid-South Conference of the United Church of Christ and a weekly contributor to talk2action.org, a web site that posts authentic research on all aspects of religious extremism, particularly Dominionism.

Their book is titled, *"Steeplejacking: How the Christian Right is Hijacking Mainstream Religion."* Here is the product description on their book and some comments about their work...

> *They describe "steeplejacking" as the takeover of churches by small groups who divide the membership, often alienating everyone but a core group. As UCC clergy they focus on congregations in their own denomination. Since UCC congregations own their own property, they are both vulnerable to steeplejacking, and they are rich prizes. In denominations like the United Methodist Church, where property belongs to the denomination itself, steeplejacking is a less viable strategy. Instead, there is a movement to split the United Methodist Church itself.*

Other reviews of this book give a summation to what Steeplejacking is about...

> *A how-to manual for progressive Christians who want to reclaim the church from intolerant, extremist factions. An important book.*
> *"[It takes] An unprecedented look inside the battle for religion in America,*

Steeplejacking: How the Christian Right is Hijacking Mainstream [mainstream] Religion" exposes how a strident theocratic minority is attacking—or "steeplejacking"-- mainstream churches in order to eliminate progressive voices and take control of America's historic mainstream denominations.

[It is] An insider account by two ministers on the front lines of mainstream religion's longtime shadow war against the religious right, <u>Steeplejacking</u> reveals how conservative renewal groups, backed by a right-wing organization called the Institute on Religion and Democracy, use social wedge issues like homosexuality to infiltrate mainstream churches and stir up dissent among members of the congregation, with the goal of taking over the leadership of the church, and ultimately, the denomination.

The book unmasks the covert methods that renewal groups and the IRD use to spread their propaganda, as well as showing how the pastor and other church leaders can act as either provocateurs or protectors in the face of an attack. Churches that have been "steeplejacked" are also examined to illustrate why some are able to withstand an attack, while others succumb.

Featuring a foreword by Michelle Goldberg , author of the bestselling *Kingdom Coming*, and an introduction by Frederick Clarkson, Steeplejacking shows how mainstream religion can fight back against the insidious tactics of the

Christian right. *-Julia Scheeres, author of*
Jesus Land: A Memoir

As you can see, calling it "steeplejacking" was not just my attempt at sarcasm. I will also add that no matter how many specific examples that can be given in their book and by firsthand accounts of those who have witnessed this practice, the good ol' "condemn and rebrand" efforts by Political Dominionists will arise as they throw their hands in the air as innocents and decry, "That wasn't us!"

Now - can you see how they used this very same method to "steeple-jack" the Republican Party?

11 The "Purpose Driven" Elephant in the Room

"What in [sic] hell scares people about talking about America's foundation of faith?" ~ Sarah Palin May 2010

I use quotes from Palin so often because her emergence onto the political stage brought religious references to a level of usage that is now viewed as "normal." Rick Warren of Saddleback Church in California wrote a book titled, "The Purpose Driven Life" that has become a manifesto for Christian living in the 21st century for Dominionists. Don't be fooled by his appearance and performance as the chosen one who gave the Invocation at President Obama's Inauguration. That is just further evidence of how unrecognized and normal their version of Christianity remains, even to someone as high up as the President.

The push to change our secular nation into one run by a religious government is relentless, and requires us to fight back in the same way. It is not a small push either; these people are determined, calculating, driven by their beliefs and their perceived mandate from God. Notice I said "driven by their beliefs." That does not always translate into truth or reality. Revising history is an integral part of the message that is disseminated to the adherents of Dominionism and other extremist views. For instance their assertion that we are a Christian Nation is, again, absolutely false. A trusted colleague explains it this way,

"Those who think religion founded the nation are incorrect. It did found many colonies. Puritans used Deuteronomy to guide their economic and social principles. All – all - prices and markets were regulated

for the best interests of the towns and their people, not the profits of the owners. Most colonies limited freedom of religion to their own church, not that of others.

The Founding Fathers drew on John Locke's secular individualism when creating the Constitution and Bill of Rights to prevent that kind of isolation, and that's what gave momentum to religious freedom, to capitalism, and to the America we have today. Religion founded colonies. Secular liberalism founded the nation." ~ Elizabeth Sholes, Director of Public Policy, California Council of Churches

A minister of the Discernment Ministries wrote a stellar summation of the relationship between Mary Glazier, Senior Apostle of the Dominionist Movement and spiritual advisor to Sarah Palin. When he refers to 'NAR' it is synonymous with those groups that dangle under the umbrella of Dominionism and means the New Apostolic Reformation. With the express written permission of Dr. Orrel Steinkamp I will share the following:

Mary Glazier: Wagner's NAR Chief Prophetess In Alaska

By Dr. Orrel Steinkamp, May 5, 2010

There is an often-repeated maxim that "you are what you eat." This is true physically and it is also just as true spiritually. What you consume as spiritual food determines who you are spiritually. I used to always be interested in seeing a pastor's theological library. A quick scan and I knew his theology and what he fed his people.

Although Palin herself has been very tight-lipped about here theological beliefs, she has left a trail of "bread-crumbs" over two decades indicating what kind of spiritual food she consumes. During the presidential campaign all the media seemed to care about was that she was a Pentecostal. But just a very little digging on the net it was clear then as now that she is much more than a Pentecostal.

I remember suggesting this to someone during the presidential election. But this was too much to swallow at the time. Indeed Sarah Palin has been linked closely to the NAR [New Apostolic Reformation] Apostolic/Prophetic Dominion Movement. Although she has tried to cover these tracks, there is ample evidence that she has been and is currently still in contact with the movement but very discretely.

Since entering national politics she has glossed over her NAR history for obvious reasons. "Since the 2008 presidential election mounting evidence suggests a dramatic widespread failure of the media to investigate and inform the American public about Sarah Palin's extensive ties to a radical, growing global movement whose leaders proclaim that an end-time army of young Christians led by Apostles and Prophets will cleanse the earth of evil and impose a Christian theocratic government." [Bruce Wilson, Talk to Action, Palin's Ties to Militant Religious Movement Confirmed]

This is now historically ironic in comparison to the wide reporting of Obama's many decades of relationship with his pastor and mentor Jeremiah Wright. But it is now time that the Christian world be informed of Palin's core apostolic/ prophetic spiritual orientation.

Wasilla AOG church and Pastor Ed Kalnins

Sarah was born Catholic but joined the Wasilla AOG along with her parents when she was 10 years old. But this AOG church is not just your traditional Pentecostal church. It became totally associated with the NAR under the ministry of Ed Kalnins. Wasilla AOG has become a major center of NAR teaching and ministry. Kalnin's sermons espouse theological concepts such as the possession of geographical areas by demonic spirits, and enter-generational transmission of family curses. [The People's Voice, Eillen Fleming, WEAREWIDEAWAKE.org] Thomas Muthee, an Apostle from Kenya visited Wasilla AOG in 2005 and there is a video online of Muthee laying apostolic hands upon Palin.

On that same occasion Muthee explained in detail the Dominion Mandate that refers to the 7 mountains of culture that need to be conquered. Muthee became famous for driving out a witch in his African hometown of Kiambu Kenya. "After 6 months of spiritual mapping Muthee came to believe that a woman known as Mama Jane was a witch and caused traffic accidents. At least one person a month would die in an accident in front of the 'divination house'. According to Muthee's account angry townsfolk wanted to stone Mama Jane for the traffic accidents. When the police entered her house they shot her pet python. She was according to Muthee questioned by the police after which she left town. This event was depicted in two videos by George Otis Jr., which Muthee claimed that the crime and traffic rate in Kiambu dropped drastically after Mama Jane left.

But the workgroup "Back to the Bible" headed by pastor Rien van de Kraats of Kamperland Netherlands found no police report or any sources that backed Muthee's claims. Investigators have asserted the Mama Jane is really Jane Njenga a local pastor who never left Kiambu [Wikipedia , Wasilla AOG].

Pastor Ed Kalnins employs all the normal prophetic practices and is on the apostolic/prophetic circuit internationally. Dutch Sheets, the top official of NAR, in the USA has visited the church on many occasions.

"Dutch Sheets was traveling (with Chuck Pierce) to Texas on Friday and when he landed in the airport his wife called and told him to get to the TV asap. He watched as McCain introduced Gov. Palin and said he began to weep, even though he knew nothing of her. He asked (Pierce?) what is the significance of this 44-year-old woman as he saw the clock said 4:44.

He asked the Lord what that was, and the Lord said...

EZ [Ezekiel] 44:4 'He brought me by way of the north gate (Alaska) to the front of the temple; so I looked, and behold, the glory of the Lord filled the house of the Lord; and I fell on my face'.

We will be having the last of our 90 days beginning in a major gathering September 11. The significance of this is that Chuck Pierce had prophesied that there would be 7 years of war and Sept. 11 marks the end of that time and entering the 8th year. 44=4+4 or 8. Dutch asked why he and Chuck were in Texas for this announcement and the Lord reminded him that the word for Texas was that it was a prophetic state. Dutch then decreed that she (Palin) will enter the White House. Now if you don't know him (Sheets) he is cautious... and never goes off half-cocked when it comes to prophecy. [Dutch Sheets on religion, politics and Sarah Palin, End Times Prophetic,WordPress.com]

Lance Wallnau, the apostolic teacher of the 7 mountains of culture has taught there recently. Wallnau is considered in the movement the foremost authority on this 7 mountains mandate and speaks on this topic almost exclusively.

Wasilla AOG has a program for recent high school graduates called the "Masters Commission', which is closely linked with Rick Joyner at Morningstar Ministries. This training program replaces the first 3 years of college. Ed Kalnins, himself, was a graduate of this program earlier. The tuition is $7900 per a year and the students are trained in prophetic gifts (learning to prophesy).

Leah L. Burton

Books by Steve Thompson head of prophetic ministry at Rick Joyner's Morningstar in Fort Mill, S.C are on the official reading list. Other books in the training program are by John Bevere who trained under Benny Hinn.

June 8, 2008, then Gov. Palin returned and spoke at the graduation ceremony of the Masters Commission at Wasilla AOG. In her speech she called for Ephesians 1:17, "that the spirit of revelation including a spirit of prophecy that God is going to tell you what is going on and what is going to go on and you guys are going to have that within you and its going to bubble up and bubble over and its going to pour out throughout Alaska." [The actual text of Ephesians 1; 17: ""I keep asking that the God of our Lord Jesus Christ, the glorious Father, may give you the Spirit of wisdom and revelation, so that you may know him better." (NIV)] There have been so many words [from NAR promoters such as prophecies by Mary Glazier] we being the head and not the tail. (Bob Fertiks Blog).

Each graduate was given a samurai sword and encouraged to prepare for warfare. In the ceremony a church member intoned: "A warriors of old were considered undressed if they were without their sword..." The church member officiating the sword ceremony then quoted Psalm 149: 6-9 "Let the high praises of God be in their throats and two edged swords in their hands to execute vengeance in the nations and punishments on the peoples, to bind their kings with chains and their nobles with fetters of iron, to execute on them the judgment written."

In 2008 Palin moved to the governor's mansion in Juneau. There she attended another AOG church, which is also more than a traditional AOG church. She attended Mike Rose's Juneau Christian Center. This church has a special relationship with Rodney Howard Brown the infamous "Holy Spirit Bartender", who dispenses "Holy Ghost Laughter." Mike Rose the pastor has had RHB visit

118

for ministry and also serves on RHB's Revival Ministries Committee. Rose also has had a long time relationship with John Hagee and his attempt to jump start the rapture.

Mary Glazier, Palin's longtime mentor and spiritual dietician

Mary Glazier was born in 1944 in Ketchikan, Alaska, the oldest of eleven. She is a Tlingit-Haida Native. She established her own ministry called Windwalkers International. She is one of the prophets of Wagner's inner circle of leadership, the Apostolic Council of Prophetic Elders ACPE. On October 8, 2008 Glazier told the attendees at the "Opening of the Gate of Heaven and Earth Conference" with many of the top leaders of the NAR in attendance, that she had been present at the inception of Sarah Palin's political career and that Palin was in her personal prayer group. (End Times Prophetic, Prophecy, Visions).

Jan Aage Torp of Oslo is an apostle in Wagner's International Coalition of Apostles. At the time of Palin's surprised nomination he was visiting with Peter Wagner and his wife Doris. He pointed out an interesting thing - that Sarah Palin is a member of the prayer network under Wagner and his Alaskan leader Mary Glazier. [End Times Prophetic, Word Press.com]

In November 17, 2009 [actually September 2008] Glazier appeared to envision (prophesy) McCain winning the 2008 election, but then being killed and soon thereafter tragically killed in a terrorist attack that would leave Palin to succeed McCain. [Huffington Post.com, Palin's Hints....] This prophetic wishful thinking turned out to be just wishful thinking.

On June 13, 2008 at a conference held at Everett, Washington, outside Seattle, Glazier describes a program of Christian religious cleansing, and the removal of unbelievers from the land. "There is a tipping point, at which, at which time, because of sin of the land the people of the land then have to be displaced.... God is preparing a people to displace the ones whose sin is rising so that they tip over and the church goes in..." (talk2action.org, Bruce Wilson, "Palins Ties to Militant Religious Movement Confirmed.)

Some of Palin's supporters have suggested that Palin no longer is in contact with Glazier. But in the January 2009 edition of Charisma Magazine in an article entitled "The Faith of Sarah Palin", authored by Lee Grady, a Wagner apostle revealed interesting details of Palin's personal continuing friendship with Alaskan Apostle and national leader Mary Glazier. In the same article it stated that "last spring Palin called Mary Glazier and asked her to pray with her over the phone, and they met [later] at the Governors Prayer Breakfast."

It seems beyond any doubt that Palin and Glazier are still in close contact. Palin obviously is still an active part of Glazier's prayer network. It also seems beyond a reasonable doubt that Palin is still consuming the teachings of the Apostolic/Prophetic Movement.

Palin, of course, represents a quantum leap potential advance for the Dominion aspirations of the NAR (refer to chapter title "The Chosen" for definition of Dominionism). She stands in a most strategic place. She stands solidly in the Apostolic Dominion Mandate of Wagner and his Apostles and Prophets. She is the darling of the Tea Party Movement, being the star speaker at their national conference. And lastly, she stands in the center of the Republican Party apparatus and seems destined to run for the office of president. **But Palin has escaped national and political scrutiny. For a still unknown reason the media gave Palin a pass.**

It seems already too late for the church and the nation to know who she is spiritually. Emotional and political emotions are deeply established. We learned more than we wanted to know about Obama. But now it's time for all to know Sarah's relationship with the NAR and especially her long mentorship under Apostle and Prophet Mary Glazier. It would be fitting that Palin disclose clearly her Glazier relationship and publicly reject the Apostolic/Prophetic dream for an American theocracy."

Contrary to those who attempt to distance Palin from Glazier, they are intertwined. In addition to Glazier, Palin has relied on the spiritual guidance and encouragements from other Dominionist leaders such as Rick Warren; Lou Engle (The Call); Apostles of C Peter Wagner such as Os Hillman, Rick Joiner and Dutch Sheets among others.

When it becomes inconvenient to be associated with these people and their extreme Bible-based views, you can't simply shake it off and deny the connections. We saw this happen when Rick Perry intentionally attempted to bury the list of endorsers in the FAQ tab of his web page that promoted his event in Houston, *"The Response"* in August 2011. Rachel Maddow did a very good story on that, highlighting this attempt to push back out of the spotlight and downplay these affiliations. It is what they do.

Here is the other clincher! These are the very same people: Lou Engle, Dutch Sheets, C Peter Wagner, John Hagee and on and on. This is no coincidence, and this is why we still need to understand Palin so we recognize the same attributes in future candidates.

Freedom vs. Theocracy

We no longer have the luxury of simple partisan politics. This is no longer Democrat vs. Republican, it is now truly Freedom vs. Theocracy. We are faced with a threat as a nation as great as anything we have seen in our 234 year history, the *marriage* of Church and State.

This is a battle for freedom versus a government based on the values and an ideology of a single religious sect, and when that happens it is known as a theocracy.

Whether we want to admit it or not this really could happen right here in America, on our own precious soil.

A theocracy is a government run on religious principles and by divine guidance, binding the citizens of that country to those values that are dictated by one single religious view. While there appears to be a conservative civil war in the making with the struggle for power and influence between the Republican Party and newly formed Tea Party, there is one thing that they all appear to hold in common with Perry, Palin, Bachmann & Co: The ongoing desire to chip away at the wall of separation of Church and State until it lies in a pile of rubble. The motivations differ but the effect of turning our government into a theocracy would generate the same results regardless of the motivation.

We cannot delude ourselves into thinking that we are immune to this threat to our freedoms The effort has already begun. Palin is simply the "poster gal." After all, it has been *clearly* demonstrated that this woman does not possess the knowledge or judgment to be a force on her own.

For myself, I want to hold on to a thread of trust that the American people would not elect a "Palin" as our President. I have to admit, though, that my confidence does waffle at times like when I stop and remind myself that it was only a few years ago that we had George W. Bush, Jr. in the White House and then my pulse quickens. But, barring a total lapse of sanity on Election Day 2012, let's focus more on the existing threats and concerns surrounding this woman and those like her that travel in that Trojan Elephant she dragged onto our national political stage in 2008.

One of the things that makes these people such a long shot to most Americans, so much so that they won't have a serious discussion about them, is that there is virtually no understanding from whence they came.

Whether it is one of the Palin, Perry, Bachmann & Co. at the helm or any of the other religious-political candidates the outcome will be the same. The erosion of our freedoms will forever change our country. It is the elimination of the minimum wage, impoverishing millions even further; the complete eradication of the middle class; the continued de-regulation of corporations, crowning them further with unbridled control; the eventual goal to privatize as much of our government as possible in a convergence of efforts and for differing reasons; the reversal of laws that presently give women control over their own bodies; the implementation of theocratic teaching in our schools; the criminalization of any relationship that is not deemed purely heterosexual. The list can – and does – go on an on.

A *"Palin's America"* is a place where freedoms are diminished and theocracy rules. It is a profoundly un-American place.

124

12 "Who's Who in the GOP 2012 Zoo?

As we watch the speculation of who will or won't run in 2012 on the Conservative side, we must look for the ones that have empirical ties to Dominionism. Right now, the following names fit that criteria and include those who have formally filed to run and those who flirt with it continuously:

Former Alaska Governor, Sarah Palin**
Texas Governor, Rick Perry**
U.S. Congresswoman, Michele Bachmann**
Former CEO of Godfather's Pizza, Herman Cain**
Former Minnesota Governor, Tim Pawlenty**

Former U.S. Senator, Rick Santorum*
Former House Speaker, Newt Gingrich*
U.S. Congressman, Ron Paul
Former Utah Governor, Jon Huntsman
Former Massachusetts Governor, Mitt Romney

** represents Dominionist candidates
*represents Ultramontane Catholics
Blank = no chance in hell of getting nominated – which include: *mainstream Christians, Mormons, Atheists, Scientologists, Buddhist, American Muslims, et al....*

This list will change before the ink is even dry on the first copy of this book, but it is important to make note of who is in the "game" at the time of this writing whether they survive or not. Some will re-emerge in later election years and as endorsers.

Mormons, Catholics and non-Born Again Protestants are not the "right kind of Christian" and will be *left_behind* in more ways than one with the rest of us who will still have our clothes on when the End of Days comes.

Not surprisingly, you will recognize a name or two in the following chapter that we have already discussed. It is an exclusive club that one must be invited to join. These are the people who bragged about "discovering" Sarah Palin.

13 Reclaiming the Seven Mountains

"You are called to preach the Gospel of the Kingdom, and the Kingdom rules over all of these mountains."
~ Lance Wallnau

Seven Mountains Mandate

The Dominionists seek to "reclaim America" through a program they refer to as the "Seven Mountains Mandate," or "Reclaiming the Seven Mountains" of culture. This goal is packaged and promoted in many forms, but Seven Mountains Mandate is a literal "product" expertly assembled and sold to congregations and converts around the globe. Here are the Seven Mountains they have articulated and claim must (in their view) "return" to the influence of Jesus Christ and be stripped from the evil clutches of secularism:

Family

Religion

Education

Media (All forms...printed, visual, audio)

Arts, Entertainment & Sports

Economy (Science, Commerce & Banking)

Government (including Military)

Their number one spokesperson and lead salesman is a fellow named, Lance Wallnau. He doesn't mince words as he states directly, "[...] only a few people in positions of authority at the top of each mountain actually determines what happens on the mountain (or area of society), thus, shaping culture." [8]

Bruce Wilson, co-founder of TalkToAction.org, a Web site dedicated to "analyzing and discussing" the religious right, said this about Palin's frighteningly extreme religious background and beliefs, making the point that they are far from apolitical:

> They're working to bring about a Christian theocratic government," Wilson said. "This is about their efforts to take control of society and government and they blatantly state their intent to do so. The seven mountains are religion, family, education, arts, media, government, and business.
> They believe that once they take full control of these seven mountains, they will be well on their way to conquering evil in the world. Assembly of God churches, such as the ones cheering Palin on all this time, call for an infiltration of Christians on each of these seven "mountains."[9]

I have personally attended teleseminars by several of the Dominionist leaders, Lance being one of them. These seminars are aggressive in their quest to capture more followers, who then gift to them in exchange for a promise of dominion and supremacy in the name of Christianity. During one presentation I had the opportunity to ask Lance and his co-host, Os Hillman, if Palin would run for President would they endorse her. Their answer was an emphatic, *"Yes!"*

The Seven Mountain Mandate will be one of those topics that will be delved into much deeper in my subsequent books, but let me share this immediately: They are intent upon having what they call the "Tipping Point" occur.

Mary Glazier and others have used this terminology. It is a mantra of the Dominionist Apostles who work under the guidance and tutelage of C. Peter Wagner, the CEO of Dominionism:

> *There is a tipping point, at which, at which time, because of the sin of the land, the people then have to be displaced. But while this measure of wickedness is rising, the measure of faith in the church is rising. God is preparing a people to displace the ones whose sin is rising so that then they tip over and the church goes in - one is removed and the church moves in and takes the territory. Now, that does not mean that the people are removed, because God removes them from the Kingdom of Darkness into the Kingdom of Light. They are given an opportunity to change allegiances." – Mary Glazier Summer of 2008 Everett, Washington.*[10]

As is often true, their own words are the best way to tell their story. The following is directly from an interview with Loren Cunningham, another prophetic apostle in the Dominionist realm:

> *It was August, 1975. My family and I were up in a little cabin in Colorado. And the Lord had given me that day a list of things I had never thought about before. He said "This is the way to reach America and nations for God. And [He said], You have to see them like classrooms or like places that were already there, and go into them with those who are already working in those areas." And I call them "mind-molders" or "spheres." I got the word "spheres" from II Corinthians 10 where*

Paul speaks in the New American Standard about the "spheres" he had been called into. And with these spheres there were seven of them, and I'll get to those in a moment. But it was a little later that day, the ranger came up, and he said, "There is a phone call for you back at the ranger's station." So I went back down, about 7 miles, and took the call. It was a mutual friend who said, "Bill Bright and Vonnette are in Colorado at the same time as you are. Would you and Darlene come over and meet with them? They would love to meet with you."

So we flew over to Boulder on a private plane of a friend of ours. And as we came in and greeted each other, {we were friends for quite a while}, and I was reaching for my yellow paper that I had written on the day before. And he said, "Loren, I want to show you what God has shown me!" And it was virtually the same list that God had given me the day before. Three weeks later, my wife Darlene had seen Dr. Francis Shaffer on TV and he had the same list! And so I realized that this was for the body of Christ.

I gave it for the first time in Hamburg, Germany at the big cathedral there to a group of hundreds of young people that had gathered at that time. And I said, "These are the areas that you can go into as missionaries. Here they are:

First, it's the institution set up by God first, the family.

After the family was church, or the people of God.

The third was the area of school, or education.

The fourth was media, public communication, in all forms, printed and electronic.

The fifth was what I call "celebration", the arts, entertainment, and sports, where you celebrate within a culture.

The sixth would be the whole area of the economy, which starts with innovations in science and technology, productivity, sales, and service. The whole area we often call it business but we leave out sometimes the scientific part, which actually raises the wealth of the world. Anything new, like making sand into chips for a microchip, that increases wealth in the world.

And so the last was the area of government. Now government, the Bible shows in Isaiah 33 verse 22 that there are three branches of government, so it's all of the three branches: judicial, legislative, and executive.

And then there are subgroups under all of those seven groups. And there are literally thousands upon thousands of subgroups. But those seven can be considered like Caleb: "Give me this mountain," and they can be a "mountain" to achieve for God. Or they can be a classroom that you're going to disciple a nation in. Because Jesus said, "Go and disciple all nations." And it also can affect us because in those areas we can be changed, transformed by the Holy Spirit to be effective missionaries into the area that God has called us into, and we will see it as not just a job to get money to stay alive, but "as the Father sent Me, so send I you," Jesus said.

[...]We began to speak it out. And today, as I fast forward to today, whenever God gave us the message, we began to speak it out and proclaim it, and then with Youth with a Mission, we began to follow what God said to do next, which was to start a university.

We call it the University of the Nations. Our first year was 1978. We set up a college, or as they call it oversees a "faculty", in all seven of the areas that was relating to each one.

Instead of setting up a college for family, but we called it counseling and healthcare in that category of family, and then we also had a school of family ministers. So, that was a part of it. And in each one of the categories we were able to do that. And from this particular basis, the Lord showed us to do it in a modular form.

Rather than one campus, we would have many campuses, multiple campuses worldwide. We presently have over 500 in 140 nations. We're offering over 800 courses and seminars and we offer courses and seminars in 82 languages now. And as they're spread around the world, this brings the university to the young people where many of them have no opportunity to go on to tertiary education. And so, this is one of the things we have continued on.

And as we are in our 29th year of the university, we're seeing about 25,000 students a year go through the university every year, and we are also moving into *another category, and that's participation with several organizations in convergence and convening; we are converging for collaboration purposes, with over 200 organizations coming together under what we call "Call to All", or you'll find it on the internet at www.call2all.org.*

As we are coming together, we're doing this in forty regions in the world, all over. We've done three already, one in the Hispanic South America, another one in Southern Africa, another one in South Pacific and Oceania which includes Australia and New Zealand. And now we are going to the rest of them throughout the nations, and as we do so, we're challenging the body of Christ to come together and having a global pastor's network, a global media network [such as Daystar, Inc.], a global educators network, and so on, using all of these spheres.

And now the church is adopting these spheres worldwide, and they're at the same time adopting what we call a map that is 4,379 locations, we call that/these are "zones", "omega zones", the name of Jesus is "Omega", [he's the alpha, the omega], and it also means "to complete."

So to complete the great commission, we want to go where we're not. Where the church isn't. Where the body of Christ isn't. Where Christians in business aren't. Where Christian educators aren't. And we want to plant all the seven spheres in all 4000 of those "Omega Zones."

And in doing so, we believe that we will forward the purpose of discipling all nations. And so this is what we're involved in right now. And it's one of those exciting times as we meet with thousands upon thousands of people around the world, and explain to them what these seven spheres are all about, and how every, literally every culture has elements of all seven spheres. So we want to be sure that Jesus, the Omega, is in every one of the spheres of the world.

Because the worldview has been shifted in America and the west. And it's been shifted away from the Biblical Christian worldview, which was in my childhood, the worldview of America, and of Europe. And then, as you see the change that has come, then we've taken on a humanistic worldview, that is basically anti-Christian. And with that, we call it a "secular worldview", [we call it "secular humanism"], but it's really against the Biblical Christian worldview. And then, that hardness of the soil is not producing anything.

And He said, "baptizing them, in the name of the son, of the father, and the Holy Ghost." How do you baptize a whole nation? They have to die to the world-view they're in. If it's a Buddhist world-view, or a Hindu world-view, and be resurrected to the world-view of the Biblical, and that which is of Jesus' world-view.

So, He will be with us to teach them all that he has taught us. And that's how you change the world-view, both in the individual, and in the world itself. You don't have to have the majority. All you have to have is the tipping point [...]

134

God, Guns & Greed

So we make whatever we do, if we do it as unto the Lord, a sanctified, or a holy work, it is Holy unto the Lord. It's not just the pulpit on Sunday, that's one of the spheres. It's also all the other spheres together, and that's how we achieve advancing the Kingdom of God."[11]

And this is their explanation of the Seven Mountains Mandate directly from their own writings, by way of leading Dominionist Apostle, Loren Cunningham, who claims to receive instruction directly from with the "big guy." [12]

The most frightening thing about this interview he gave (you can watch on YouTube or read it on the internet, by the way) is how widespread his followers are. This is why they must be taken seriously as well as the candidates they support. Through programs like "Market Place Leaders" and "Reclaiming the Seven Mountains" these Dominionists are gathering new supporters and accumulating tremendous wealth along the way.

Loren Cunningham is the founder of Youth with a Mission (YWAM) that is responsible for harvesting millions of souls on college campuses worldwide into this bible-based cult of Dominionism based on his frequent prophecies and poolside chit-chats with J.C.

14 Reclaim, Revise, Rewrite, Restore, Reagan, Revival, Reformation & Redux!

"This new conservatism appeals to the hearts of the mindless and the minds of the heartless" ~ unknown

Reclaim

This is all a shell game. Nothing has been taken away from these people, but they are convinced that America is no longer what it once was: – A Christian nation of all white people who belong to the same churches and are the only ones patriotic enough to display the American flag. They have convinced themselves and each other that their very existence is threatened and that there is something in need of "reclaiming." (Of course, none of this is due at all to the fact that we have our very first Africa-American President in the White House.)

So who makes up this voting-bloc? The bulk of them are those who consider themselves to be the "true" patriotic conservative Christians in America. They are joined by a smattering of enthusiastic (albeit a touch paranoid) gun owner/anti-government/secessionists types and topped off with self-interested, uber-wealthy corporate fat cats whose "generosity" created the Tea Party.

Ergo – *God, Guns & Greed.*

And now, here we *all* are - stuck in the middle of their Three Ring Circus replete with clown show! Those of us who are worried must look in the mirror and admit that in most cases, we didn't see it coming. We didn't read the warning signs going back to the eighties.

These people may be a minority, they are an angry and loud mob who are fed a 24/7 I.V. drip of constant fear and paranoia. If only they had felt this patriotic during the Bush years when we were being flushed down the drain pipe as a country, toward economic disaster.

One reporter put it this way:

> *"We'll likely never be offered an explanation from Sarah's [Palin's] voting bloc, as to why they chose to sit on their hands while the Bush-Cheney Administration decimated the Constitution and Bill of Rights, and plundered our economy to historic depths (driving our country to its knees, creating massive unemployment, bank failures, the demise of businesses, bankruptcy, foreclosures, hunger, homelessness, etc.) but yet were inspired to fight to the death for America last fall...." [on the heels of the Health Care debate in 2009]*

Indeed, where were they?

Authoritarians Reminiscent of Playground Bullies

In a nutshell we have some very loud, aggressive unhappy people in this country who cannot find contentment. They are those that insist that everyone must think, do and *be* just like them. If you're not, they'd prefer that you just disappear. This is, at its essential level, the most unpatriotic and un-American attitude that any of us can have.

We are about freedom of thought, speech and belief. This country is not about majority rule. It is about democracy and fairness. But there is no engaging the fringe of the angry Right. Neither is there any use reasoning with those who may or may not be play-acting while getting paid millions to cater to those that truly feel this angst. They – don't – care! Period.

They just want to be in charge and force the rest of us to play by their rules. Whether it is Rush Limbaugh, Sean Hannity, Bill O'Reilly, Glenn Beck, Sarah Palin, and all the other ranting and whipped-up conservative media spokespersons, they cannot avoid the temptation to use name-calling and degrading verbiage when talking about opposing viewpoints. They are bullies.

This not only gets us absolutely nowhere in this country in terms of solving the real problems that most of us are facing in our daily lives, but it is an international embarrassment. I am ashamed of the rhetoric that is so disrespectful across the board by these extreme "Righties," but never so much as when they disrespect the President of our United States and horribly and rudely berate our First Lady and their family. This is childish and profoundly inexcusable, yet it never stops.

There is an eye-popping book available written by a man named Bob Altemeyer titled, *"The Authoritarians,"* and he is spot on about the type of personalities that are drawn to this Movement. He is a Professor of Psychology from the University of Manitoba in Winnipeg, Canada and has even made it available online as a free download.[13] This is in incredibly valuable resource in assisting to understand their minds, and I encourage all my readers to download it and read it.

He warns that, even though we can surely avoid a Dominionist president if everyone that feels strongly about the issue simply makes the effort to vote, we are not out of the woods. He wrote these words pre-Palin:

"But even if their leaders cannot find an acceptable presidential candidate for 2008 [2012], even if authoritarians play a much diminished role in the next election, even if they temporarily fade from view, they will be there, aching for a dictatorship that will force their views on everyone. And they will surely be energized again, as they were in 1994, if a new administration infuriates them while carrying out its mandate. The country is not out of danger yet."

It is almost chilling to read his words vis à vis what has transpired in the very recent past. He goes on to share research results and interviews with participants who hold dogmatic religious views and discusses how those become volatile when blended with politics. There is an amazing amount of very thought-provoking information laid out in an easy to read format. In an effort to describe for us a way to understand the fear and paranoia that plague these folks he asks that we go back in our memory and remember how we all felt within minutes, hours, days, weeks and even months after 9/11.

Professor Altemeyer says that this is the level of fear and paranoia that they live with every day – **and it is completely real to them**.

Revisionist Rewrites

People like Glenn Beck, himself a Mormon, clearly hasn't a clue that he is being used to further their purposes just like the angry "sheeples" who tune in to listen to his crazed ranting. Mormons are, as I have pointed out a few times in this book, "not the right kind of Christian." He is a "tool" (that is what they call me in the never-ending hate mail that I receive) and is being played by these people.

It is so blatant to those of us who study Dominionism and watch their next move, that the most glaring move of the past couple of years was when David Barton sidled up to Beck and used Beck's ability to reach a vast audience so Barton could spread his 100% revisionist history of America.

David Barton is a friend and associate of 2012 Presidential candidate Michele Bachmann's and he has been at this for a very long time. He travels the country giving "shows" to people that lap up every false morsel of information that he disseminates. In 2012, after the Republicans took the majority in the House of Representatives, Michele Bachmann appointed David Barton to give tours to congressional members as their trusted "historian."14 Barton finds proof everywhere that God made the United States in His image.

Barton is no historian, and even though he holds zero accreditations that indicate any serious study in American History, both of his pals former Arkansas Governor and 2008 presidential candidate Mike Huckabee and the very emotionally fragile Glenn Beck actually call Barton, "The Library of Congress in shoes." 15

From Texas, Barton grew up in a very conservative Christian home and served as a youth director at his father's Aledo Christian School, an institution affiliated with a the church of the same name, which was started by his parents. He does possess a bachelor of arts in religious education at Oral Roberts University (what other type of education is there at ORU?) in 1976. This is the same institution that actually gave Bachmann a degree in law.

Our Senior Researcher at the Military Religious Freedom Foundation is a woman named Chris Rodda. She has gone toe-to-toe and head-to-head with Barton for years refuting with evidence what can be called nothing other than fabricated lies. But where better to peddle that kind of fiction than FOX?

Rodda wrote a book titled, "Liars for Jesus" and has worked tirelessly for a very little compensation in her efforts to combat this proselytizing in the military and education. She takes it personally when these false claims are sucked up by the uninformed audiences who watch the likes of Glenn Beck. I highly recommend her book.

And if you question whether or not they are being successful, please go and look up what happened in Texas during the Spring of 2010. The Texas Board of Education has made progress in their effort to re-write history. And because they are such major purchasers of textbooks in the U.S., their input dictates what the rest of the country's school children are subjected to.

Dominionists view public education as "institutions of Satan" and they will not rest until they have destroyed the public education system in America. Proposed changes to the textbooks in this major victory for Dominionists reported by The New York Times March 2012 included[16]:

*Insist students learn about the conservative resurgence the 1980s and 1990s including Phyllis Schlafly

*Include The Contract with America, The Heritage Foundation, The Moral Majority, and the National Rifle Association

*Remove Ted Kennedy and replace with Newt Gingrich

*Remove Thomas Jefferson and replace with St. Thomas Aquinas, John Calvin and William Blackstone (because Jefferson coined the term "separation of Church and State" and wrote the Virginia Act for Establishing Religious Freedom).

Restore America ~ A Tea Party Mandate

All of this contributes to the performances by celebrities like Glenn Beck's "Restore America" rally in Washington, D.C. in 2010. The performance on the steps of the Lincoln Memorial capped off the summer with Glenn Beck in the role of emcee and self-proclaimed leader of the movement to save America from the grasp of communism/socialism/fascist/secularism and evil progressives! He was joined in this goat-rope by none other than our gal Sarah who showed up to stir the crowd and rally up the troops, in protest of everything that actually allowed her to stand before this crowd and protest.

Their message was riddled with anti-government sentiment even though many of their top proponents are either in government, or striving to get there! Michelle Bachmann who calls herself a member of the Tea Party is really suffering from an identity-crisis and is just one example of an elected career politician, who constantly repeats anti-government rhetoric such as this:

> "*I want people in Minnesota armed and dangerous on this issue of the energy tax because we need to fight back. Thomas Jefferson told us 'having a revolution every now and then is a good thing,' and the people -- we the people -- are going to have to fight back hard if we're not going to lose our country." - Rep. Michele Bachmann (R), March 2009*
>
> *...and, "I wish the American media would take a great look at the views of the people in Congress and find out: Are they pro-America or anti-America?" -Rep. Michelle Bachmann (R), calling for a new McCarthyism, Oct. 2008*
>
> *...as if she wasn't a member of that body. And then there is this inflammatory remark that just fuels the fires of the fearful and paranoid who already think their government is after them:*
>
> *Take this into consideration. If we look at American history, between 1942 and 1947, the data that was collected by the Census Bureau was handed over to the FBI*

and other organizations at the request of President Roosevelt, and that's how the Japanese were rounded up and put into the internment camps. I'm not saying that that's what the Administration is planning to do, but I am saying that private personal information that was given to the Census Bureau in the 1940s was used against Americans to round them up, in a violation of their constitutional rights, and put the Japanese in internment camps" - Rep. Michele Bachmann (R), June 2009

...and finally, just to put her statements into context for us she confesses this,

I look at the Scripture and I read it and I take it for what it is. I give more credence in the Scripture as being kind of a timeless word of God to mankind, and I take it for what it is. And I don't think I give as much credence to my own mind, because I see myself as being very limited and very flawed, and lacking in knowledge and wisdom and understanding. So, I just take the Bible for what it is, I guess, and recognize that I am not a scientist, not trained to be a scientist. I'm not a deep thinker on all of this. I wish I was. I wish I was more knowledgeable, but I'm not a scientist. - Michele Bachmann interviewing with Todd Fiel at KKMS. as quoted in the Stillwater Gazette, September 29, 2003.

I have quoted Bachmann here to demonstrate that it isn't all about Sarah, as disappointing as that news may be to Palin. There are many, many who are sharing these outrageous worldviews who are politicians – elected or running. And the extremists have identified themselves synonymously with the very far Right.

We can't transition from here without at least a quote or two from Texas Governor Rick Perry like this one who thinks that only God can fix the government, *"God, you are gonna have to fix this."* Or this one where he threatened to secede from the Union,

> *"Texas is a unique place. When we came into the union in 1845, one of the issues was that we would be able to leave if we decided to do that," Perry said. "My hope is that America and Washington in particular pays attention. We've got a great union. There's absolutely no reason to dissolve it. But if Washington continues to thumb their nose at the American people, who knows what may come of that."*

And just one other, there are SO many to choose from!

> *We've got the wind at our back right now. Americans are waking up to the realities of their previous choices. We must keep America moving back to preeminence because our values and conservative ideas are the world's greatest hope.*

Reagan would be a Blue Dog Dem to these Republicans Today!

If Ronald Reagan were alive today, as much as they love to embrace him as their ideal Republican icon, he would be too liberal for these folks. Cenk Uygar made these observations while hosting the Dylan Ratigan Show on MSNBC in 2009:

Ronald Reagan:
- gave amnesty to illegal immigrants.

- negotiated with terrorists. (He traded arms for hostages with Iran.)

- raised taxes on large scale four times. (He did this after initially lowering them.)

- negotiated with the "evil empire" without preconditions.

- made a decision to "cut and run" from Lebanon after our troops were attacked there.

"In fact, as you look at the Reagan list, it seems he is the exact opposite of what conservatives now claim they want. It looks like the caricature of what they think liberals do. There is no way that even Dennis Kucinich would be able to do all of those things; he certainly wouldn't negotiate with terrorists the way Reagan did. [...] the political line has moved so far that if Reagan tried to run as a Republican now he would be the laughing stock of the party. Rush Limbaugh would tear him to shreds and Bill Kristol would say he is Neville Chamberlain. He would be run out of town as a tax-raising, amnesty giving, terrorist negotiating, cut and run no-good lib who hates the troops.

And anyone who claims otherwise is being absurd. As Reagan once said, 'Facts are stubborn things.'" ~ Cenk Uygar

Of course, Reagan also took the country further right in many ways but our political spectrum has moved so much further to the right that he looks left behind by comparison.

According to Ron Reagan, Jr.: ~ <u>YOU</u> Madam "are NO Ronald Reagan!" Or ARE you?

In response to one of the many little nasty-grams shot toward Sarah Palin from Karl Rove (quoted by the Telegraph, a British newspaper), Rove suggested that her reality show on TLC would hurt her chances in 2012. Palin's reaction was to suggest that her Discovery Channel show, *"Palin's Alaska"* was not to be compared to a reality TV show. Rather she insisted that considering her show a documentary was a far more credible way to think of it. Palin responded by saying that it does not, *"hurt her chances in a 2012 presidential run because President Ronald Reagan was also an entertainer."*

Rove went on to say,

> With all due candor, appearing on your own reality show on the Discovery Channel, I am not certain how that fits in the American calculus of 'that helps me see you in the Oval Office.'
>
> There are high standards that the American people have for it [the presidency] and they require a certain level of gravitas, and they want to look at the candidate and say 'that candidate is doing things that gives me confidence that they are up to the most demanding job in the world.'

Fox News' Chris Wallace asked Palin to respond to Rove:

> "You know, I agree with that [...], those standards have to be high for someone who would ever want to run for

*president like, um, wasn't Ronald Reagan
an actor? Wasn't he in Bedtimes for Bonzo,
bozo or something? Ronald Reagan was an
actor.*

Okay. Puh-*lease*! So what does his own flesh and blood and namesake think about these sporadic comparisons of herself to President Reagan?

Asked in an interview on the Joy Behar Show, a talk show on HLN channel, Ron Reagan, Jr. had this exchange when Joy brought up Sarah Palin.

Behar: "Why would your father NOT like this woman?"

Ron, Jr: *"Because she doesn't have a thought in her head! My father knew what he stood for – you can disagree with him or not. He knew what he stood for. He could explain what he stood for. While he was conversant in foreign and domestic policy – she's neither! She can't explain where she stands on anything!"*

But let's look at what Sarah Palin, Rick Perry, Michele Bachmann, Mike Huckabee (and others) do share with President Ronald Reagan, in ways that *can* be directly compared. It would be their End Times theology, their belief that we are living in the age of Armageddon and if that means bringing the entire world to its knees to get there – so be it. World War III. It is this likeness to Reagan that they hold deep inside and then confidently use that self-knowledge to deflect any notion that they are not the chosen ones to carry on in his footsteps.

All the way back in the infancy stage of the American political Dominionist Movement in 1984, Reagan was President of the United States and those that recognized his alarming remarks about a "nuclear Armageddon" were a tiny minority. Eleven times between 1968 and 1984 Reagan referred to the world coming to an end in Biblical terms. Time magazine reported this November 5, 1984:

In one of the most peculiar twists of the 1984 campaign, St. John's apocalyptic vision of the "End Times" emerged last week as a political issue. During the final presidential debate, Panelist Marvin Kalb of NBC asked Ronald Reagan, "Do you feel that we are now heading, perhaps, for some kind of nuclear Armageddon?" While Nancy Reagan gasped, "Oh, no!" to companions, the President answered that, yes, he had chatted with people about "the biblical prophecies of what would portend the coming of Armageddon and so forth, and the fact that a number of theologians for the last decade or more have believed that this was true, that the prophecies are coming together that portend that.

-Richard N. Ostling, Time Magazine

Here are a smattering of other comments Reagan made about the End Times and Armageddon. In a 1980 interview with Jim Bakker, said, "We may be the generation that sees Armageddon." Before that, in 1971, Reagan commented to James Mills regarding events in Libya, "For the first time ever, everything is in place for the Battle of Armageddon and the Second Coming of Christ."

Obviously, Reagan thought that the end would come SOON! One writer said, "And to think that a man with apocalyptic delusions like this had his finger on the nuclear button for 8 years."

So do we disagree with Ron Reagan Jr? Look at these bullet points of direct Reagan quotes, quotes from those who worked near him and with him and a couple of his presidential policy facts:

"A faceless mass, waiting for handouts." Ronald Reagan, 1965. (Reagan describing Medicaid recipients.)

"Unemployment insurance is a pre-paid vacation for freeloaders." California Governor Ronald Reagan, in the Sacramento Bee, April 28, 1966

"I never knew anything above Cs." President Reagan, in a moment of truthfulness, describes his academic record to Barbara Walters, November 27, 1981

"They told stories about how inattentive and inept the President was.... They said he wouldn't come to work--all he wanted to do was to watch movies and television at the residence." Jim Cannon (an aide to Howard Baker) reporting what Reagan's underlings told him, Landslide: The Unmaking of the President: 1984-88

"Reagan's only contribution [to the subject of the MX missile] throughout the entire hour and a half was to interrupt somewhere at midpoint to tell us he'd watched a movie the night before, and he gave us the plot from War Games, the movie. That was his only contribution." Lee Hamilton (Representative from Indiana) interviewed by Haynes Johnson, *Sleepwalking Through History: America in the Reagan Years*:

> *This President is treated by both the press and foreign leaders as if he were a child.... It is major news when he honors a political or economic discussion with a germane remark and not an anecdote about his Hollywood days. - Columnist Richard Cohen*

"He demonstrated for all to see how far you can go in this life with a smile, a shoeshine and the nerve to put your own spin on the facts." - David Nyhan, Boston Globe columnist

"An amiable dunce." - Clark Clifford (former Defense Secretary)

"Poor dear, there's nothing between his ears." - British Prime Minister Margaret Thatcher

"Like reinventing the wheel." - Larry Speakes (Reagan's former press secretary) describing what it was like preparing the President for a press conference,

Speaking Out: The Reagan Presidency from Inside the White House

"The task of watering the arid desert between Reagan's ears is a challenging one for his aides." - Columnist David Broder

"He has the ability to make statements that are so far outside the parameters of logic that they leave you speechless." - Patti Davis (formerly Patricia Ann Reagan) talking about her father, *The Way I See It*

"This loathing for government, this eagerness to prove that any program to aid the disadvantaged is nothing but a boondoggle and a money gobbler, leads him to contrive statistics and stories with unmatched vigor." Mark Green, *Reagan's Reign of Error*

"President Reagan doesn't always check the facts before he makes statements, and the press accepts this as kind of amusing." - former president Jimmy Carter, March 6, 1984

"Approximately 80 percent of our air pollution stems from hydrocarbons released by vegetation. So let's not go overboard in setting and enforcing tough emission standards for man-made sources." –Ronald Reagan, quoted in Sierra, September 10, 1980

"I've said it before and I'll say it again. The U.S. Geological Survey has told me that the proven potential for oil in Alaska alone is greater than the proven reserves in Saudi Arabia." --Ronald Reagan, quoted in the *Detroit Free Press*, March 23, 1980. (According to the USGS, the Saudi reserves of 165.5 billion barrels are 17 times the proven reserves--9.2 billion barrels--in Alaska.)

"Why should we subsidize intellectual curiosity?" - Ronald Reagan, campaign speech, 1980

"We think there is a parallel between federal involvement in education and the decline in profit over recent years." -President Reagan, quoted in *USA Today*, April 26, 1983

"What we have found in this country, and maybe we're more aware of it now, is one problem that we've had, even in the best of times, and that is the people who are sleeping on the grates, the homeless who are homeless, you might say, by choice." - President Reagan, defending himself against charges of callousness on *Good Morning America*, January 31, 1984

"I would have voted against the Civil Rights Act of 1964." --Ronald Reagan, *Los Angeles Times*, June 17, 1966

"Today a newcomer to the state is automatically eligible for our many aid programs the moment he crosses the border." - Ronald Reagan, in a speech announcing his candidacy for Governor, January 3, 1966. (In fact, immigrants to California had to wait five years before becoming eligible for benefits. Reagan acknowledged his error, but nine months later said exactly the same thing.)

"[Not] until now has there ever been a time in which so many of the prophecies are coming together. There have been times in the past when people thought the end of the world was coming, and so forth, but never anything like this." - President Reagan revealing a disturbing view about the "coming of Armageddon," December 6, 1983

"Politics is just like show business. You have a hell of an opening, coast for a while, and then have a hell of a close." - Ronald Reagan to aide Stuart Spencer, 1966

FACTS:

The Reagan administration had secret plans for an unconstitutional takeover of the federal government under an ill-defined national emergency. Members of the government created by the coup had been selected and included Richard Cheney.[17]

The claim that Reagan won the Cold War is pure rightwing propaganda. The Soviet Union had long been far weaker than many American leaders knew, or wished to acknowledge, thanks to CIA gross overestimates of its economy. The Soviet Union was brought down by a number of factors including the inherent weaknesses of dictatorship and ethnic divides that eventually forced its breakup.[18]

Bill Press - "It was Reagan who first proposed a missile defense system -- immediately dubbed "Star Wars" by skeptical reporters -- in a March 23, 1983 speech from the Oval Office. However, as Frances Fitzgerald reveals in her brilliant history Way Out There in the Blue, Reagan didn't get his plan from the scientists or the generals. The Pentagon wasn't even notified of his speech ahead of time. Reagan stole Star Wars directly from -- the movies.[19]

In 1940, appearing in the Warner Brothers thriller "Murder in the Air," Reagan played an American secret agent charged with protecting a super weapon that could strike all enemy planes from the air. Then in 1966, Alfred Hitchcock released a Reagan favorite, "Torn Curtain," in which American agent Michael Armstrong (played by Paul Newman) works on developing an anti-missile missile. In words that must have made Ronnie tingle, Newman's character asserts: "We will produce a defensive weapon that will make all nuclear weapons obsolete, and thereby abolish the terror of nuclear warfare." Sound familiar? Reagan used almost the exact words in selling missile defense from the office, 17 years later.

Desmond Tutu to Reagan on Apartheid: "In my view, the Reagan administration's support and collaboration with it is equally immoral, evil, and totally un-Christian. . . . You are either for or against apartheid and not by rhetoric. You are either in favor of evil or you are in favor of good. You are either on the side of the oppressed or on the side of the oppressor. You can't be neutral."

The former actor and California governor offended blacks when he kicked off his 1980 general election campaign by promoting "states rights" (once southern code for "segregation") in Philadelphia, Miss., scene of the murder of three civil rights workers 16 years before.

The combination of a huge "supply-side" tax cut, a historic military buildup and a painful two-year recession produced huge budget deficits and a near tripling of the national debt that haunted the country and policymakers for years and drained resources from social programs.

Now go back and look at these, which only represent a fraction of quotes and comments about President Reagan, and replace his name with Perry's, Palin's, Bachmann's, DeMint's or any number of these same End Times obsessed zealots and tell me that they aren't a chip off the ol' Reagan block. McCain started the comparison right after their resounding defeat when asked about Palin as she flitted about on her first book tour,

> When asked about Palin's new book and her political future McCain said, 'I read I think she's keeping her options open, and I think she should. I think she is an incredible force in the American political arena.' McCain went on to compare her divisiveness to Ronald Reagan, 'I think that anybody who has the visibility that Sarah has is obviously going to have some divisiveness. I remember that a guy named Ronald Reagan used to be viewed by some as divisive.' He concluded by lavishing more praise on Palin, 'I think she's doing a great job. I think she's doing a great job. I think she has motivated our base. I think she had a positive impact on the last election, and I'm proud of her'. ~ Jason Easley, PoliticusUSA.com

Same smell, different garbage...

Revival, Reformation, Redux

The "Re" words just keep coming. It is interesting how these folks who claim to be the "real Americans" are the ones who want to profoundly change this country into a place that our founding fathers and all those who gave their lives to defend our freedoms and unique way of life would not unrecognizable.

15 The March of the Theocrats: Embedded Inequality

The protester said, "I'm born again. I can do anything I want." ~a firsthand encounter told by Elizabeth Sholes

The following chapter is written by Elizabeth Sholes, a remarkable woman who has fought against Dominionism on the side of mainstream Christians for decades. Her wisdom and insight are invaluable in putting together how this is a concerted effort to use the power of the courts, legislative process and unknowing church congregations to embed inequality into America's Rule of Law.

Outside a women's clinic, the usual back-and-forth between anti-abortion protesters and clinic defense people was occurring when one of the anti-abortion protesters, in a fit of rage, whirled on the pro-choice folks and yelled, "Fuck off!" The pro-choice people, in feigned shock, said, "Well! That's not a very Christian thing to say!" The protester said, "I'm born again. I can do anything I want."

Another protester, frustrated at not being able to convert the liberal pro-choice people, hurled the ultimate threat: "I'm going to Heaven and you're not!"

Dominionist adherents in their absolute superiority as the "Elect" would be irrelevant were it confined to a personal religious belief. Americans largely have a time-honored "live and let live" attitude about other people's religious views and faith. Americans have never had religious wars or even intense segregation based on religion. Broadly speaking, and over simplified, there are two strands of Christianity that have co-existed reasonably peacefully in America sometimes working in concert, sometimes not, but generally operating in an arena of mutual tolerance - if not acceptance.

Mainstream Protestantism and Catholicism have tended to be focused on the teachings of Christ that led numerous denominations to follow the "Social Gospel" of both charity for those in immediate need and pursuit of justice to alter social conditions. This view upholds the Common Good – the general welfare of the Constitution – as the paramount societal and political goal. Respecting religious diversity, embracing human equality, and seeking economic and political freedom for all are inherent faith values from which mainstream denominations come to promote core democratic values.

Conservative Christianity on the other hand puts primacy on salvation of one's soul. That, in turn, puts emphasis on personal responsibility for one's entire life condition. Charity may be something one gives now and then, but it is not a function for government since that would coddle those in need and deter them from finding Jesus, being saved, and altering their own lives for the better.

While both strands of faith were active in early America and in movements such as abolition, after the Civil War conservative Christianity moved frequently to embrace business and business people and to turn from nascent labor, women's, and civil rights movements, seeing them as violations of Biblical laws.

Intensely conservative parts of the movement such as "The Fellowship" noted in Jeff Sharlet's book, *The Family*, grew from its founder's violent rejection of the 20th century labor movement that he believed violated the tenets of Christianity. Businessmen were the "natural" leaders since, in the Family's view, the Apostles had been businessmen. Labor was to be obedient and subservient, not strike out on their own as equals. Women, minorities, immigrants – all were subordinated to the business community's interests not in just material, cultural, and class ideology but as manifestations of Christian values.

When the personal turns political, when religious views become grounds for policy, then it becomes a concern for all Americans. Jockeying for policy control is as old as the nation, and it would raise no eyebrows if these were ordinary times, ordinary people. However, since 1964 after the defeat of Barry Goldwater and especially since the 1980s, the Religious Right has sought power to impose its agenda. Not content to simply have different perspectives as the traditional parties do, the Religious Right brokered Ronald Reagan's presidential hopes by demanding, and getting the GOP to adopt a narrow agenda of ten items ranging from making abortion and gay rights non-existent to assuring tax breaks for the wealthy and corporations.

Dominionism is the Religious Right on Steroids

Given the dovetailing with corporate interests, it was a match made, if not in Heaven, certainly in the Party platform. The Religious Right, growing more rigid by the year, has dictated Republican policy since 1980. The intensification of control by Dominionists has swept even traditional conservative Christians out of the way. When Evangelicals in Alabama led "Alabama Arise" to reform that state's highly regressive state tax code, it was the Christian Coalition that rose in vigorous opposition. For them, like Leona Helmsley, "only the little people" should pay taxes.

As Dominionism increases its political hold, much of the Tea Party, including the governors and many legislators, are Dominionists or silent allies. It is not enough to win seats or control houses in Congress, one must pass a religious litmus test and the results had best show that they are the "right kind of Christian."

Today the goal is to transform the very institutions of government in order to create a structure of embedded inequality. Dominionists don't just want their policy goals, they want to command all of the structures of our society to govern not from democratic principle but from the Bible. Those who are not true believers, who are not "born again" or "saved" cannot, in their view, have the same rights as those who follow a very specific view of Jesus and God's laws. This is demonstrated in this statement from the Director of Issue Analysis for the American Family Association...

> *Islam has no fundamental First Amendment claims, for the simple reason that it was not written to protect the religion of Islam. Islam is entitled only to the religious liberty we extend to it out of courtesy. While there certainly ought to be a presumption of religious liberty for non-Christian religious traditions in America, the Founders were not writing a suicide pact when they wrote the First Amendment. - Bryan Fischer, AFA*

Though this targets Islam, his reference is clear – that non-Christians in the United States are allowed to be here and worship as a privilege – not a right under the Fourth Amendment. There is a reason why AFA is now considered a "hate group" under the criteria of the Southern Poverty Law Center, not the least of which include Fischer's open remarks, writings and verbal attacks on Native Americans, African Americans, Muslims, gays and Hispanics.

The centuries-old separation of church and state is eroding via changes to state and federal laws. Nowhere is that more clear than in the school board fights over incorporating "intelligent design" into the curriculum, or in Supreme Court rulings that are destroying that separation. Again, this begs a quote from Fischer from July 14, 2011...

> *Of course the main problem with that mission statement is that the "separation between church and state" is not a constitutional principle at all. You will look in vain for the phrase "separation of church and state" anywhere in the document created by the Founders. You could have found it in the constitution of the old Soviet Union, which ought to tell you something, but it's just not in our founding document at all.*
>
> *Now there is a wall there, but it is not between church and state. It is a high and impenetrable wall between the state and the church. The state is forbidden by the First Amendment from meddling in the affairs of the church. It can't tell it what to believe, how to worship, what to pray, or what to preach from its pulpits.*
>
> *But there is nothing in the Constitution that prohibits the church from impacting the state, whether it does so by speaking truth to political power, or by advancing its cherished moral ideals in the public square.*

These goals are no longer simply the hopes and dreams of zealous religio-political Dominionists; they are an American political reality, in large part due to the total redefining of what "conservative" means in American politics today.

We see the growing sense of Dominionist entitlement every day as many are convinced that to hold opposing view makes you what they tout now as an evil secular humanist.

Sarah Leslie's article, "Dominionism and the Rise of Christian Imperialism", notes that over the past four decades, the various strands of Dominionism have united to produce a global "Kingdom agenda" – "a **literal and physical Kingdom** to be advanced on earth in the present age."

She cites Al Dager in his book, "*Vengeance is Ours: The Church in Dominion:*

> *Dominion theology is predicated upon three basic beliefs:*
>
> *1) Satan usurped man's dominion over the earth through the temptation of Adam and Eve;*
>
> *2) The Church is God's instrument to take dominion back from Satan;*
>
> *3) Jesus cannot or will not return until **the Church** has taken dominion **by gaining control of the earth's governmental and social institutions**.* [emphasis added by Leslie.]

They want to take over governmental institutions for their own agenda, for their own representation, for their own self interest, not for the good of the nation. From the Texas revisionist history texts that downplay not only slavery but the accomplishments of minorities and women, the march of the theocrats is everywhere. Their beliefs to which they are entitled as matters of their own faith, are now being promulgated as public policy.

Most fearful of all is the rolling back of the Social Contract, the intentional march to destroy social programs upon which the vast majority of Americans rely; Medicare, Social Security and Medicaid for those in need and especially our elders. Public education is a way of life for our children and publicly funded higher education for our youth, but education in particular is being aggressively targeted. All of these are under relentless attack by Dominionist political theology that rejects equal opportunity and equality itself as inherent American rights.

The political assaults on unions is to prevent not just the amassing of equal political power by working people, but the very right of people to gather together to speak for their own well being. Corporate capital – the gathering together of investors – is fine. Unity among employees violates the "natural order" of Biblical hierarchy. It is not just conservative anti-union ideology behind the attack on public employees. The governors of Michigan, Wisconsin, Ohio and other states elected in 2010 are all Dominionists who have adopted the embedded inequality of that faith view and are making it manifest in public policy.

Most worrisome of all are recent Supreme Court decisions. Recent decisions, often found on narrow 5-4 splits, are beginning to enshrine permanent embedded inequality in our laws. The decisions have not only given powerful interests greater rights than individuals, they have put collective private rights ahead of collective public ones.

Citizens United v. The Federal Elections Commission argues that money was free speech and that corporations, as fictitious persons, could campaign without limits. Thus, a fictitious person has more rights than a real one that is still restricted in campaign dollars. In McComish v. Bennett the majority ruled that the state of Arizona could no longer match the funds for a publicly funded candidate to equal the spending of a privately funded candidate. In a remarkably peculiar decision, the majority declared that providing matching funds would have a "chilling effect" on free speech while the dissenting justices noted that public funds equaling private ones would certainly increase free speech. This ruling is more about curtailing the use of public dollars than about speech.

Religious equality and government neutrality are being violated with growing frequency. In Arizona,

Christian School Tuition Organization v. Kathleen Winn et al., the majority ruled that the tax credit given by CSO – discriminatory on its face – for religious (ultra conservative) education could not be appealed by taxpayers since it's a credit not an appropriation so, previous rulings to the contrary, it does not violate the Establishment Clause. But not only does a credit given for religious education promote specific religion, taxpayer challenges are ruled illegitimate.

Class action lawsuits were put in jeopardy by the Wal-Mart ruling that declared that workplace decisions were made individually - which, of course, they are not- thereby throwing thousands of poor and low income women back to re-file – hire a lawyer and pay their own legal costs – if they ever to hope to see justice done on their behalf.

The decision was compounded by Justice Antonin Scalia's earlier declaration that, the Fourteenth Amendment on citizen rights notwithstanding, **the United States Constitution does not protect women.** Corporations have protection. People do not. In fact, his quote, prefaced with a smarmy, "Sorry to tell you this," when he stated that the Constitution does not protect women or gay Americans from discrimination. He went on to say,

> *"You do not need the Constitution to reflect the wishes of the current society. Certainly the Constitution does not require discrimination on the basis of sex. The only issue is whether it prohibits it. It doesn't. Nobody ever thought that that's what it meant. Nobody ever voted for that. If the current society wants to outlaw discrimination by sex, hey we have things called legislatures, and they enact things called laws."- October 2010*

The Fourteenth Amendment to the Constitution -- equal protection under the law -- does not apply to sex discrimination, Scalia said in a recent interview

Using the instruments of our Constitution to give preference to religious conservatives and their corporate allies shapes a new America, one of declining equality, rising hierarchies and preferences.

Theocrats on the march mean that someday we may be like Orwell's Animal Farm where everyone is equal – **but some are more equal than others.**

16 "All of 'em, _Any_ of 'em"

"America will never be destroyed from the outside. If we falter and lose our freedoms, it will be because we destroyed ourselves." ~ **ABRAHAM LINCOLN**

Dominionists – Constitutionalists – Corporatists

Many, many groups, political organizations and ideological partnerships have formed over the years, frequently causing a blurring of the lines when these forces are joined to achieve common goals. Some of the oddest cross-pollinization has resulted including the curious camaraderie of the following:

- o Secessionists;
- o "Christian Zionists" and Jewish Zionist groups
- o Ultramontane (fundamentalist) Catholic groups such as the Sovereign Order of Malta and Opus Dei;
- o "Old Order Catholic" schismatic groups not recognized by the Roman Catholic Church;
- o neo-Libertarians;
- o Constitution Party (Howard Phillips III – the fast track to Dominionism);
- o Joe McArthyism;
- o anti-"New World Order" conspiracy theorists (such as Michelle Bachmann) who worry that the census will come out & Obama will send UN soldiers to knock on

166

doors and round up people based on race or religion—in part playing on US history of rounding up First Nations peoples, Japanese internment camps, and leaked Oliver North-authored plan "Rex 84" (FEMA exercise in event of mass "Black Nationalist" uprising);

o tax evaders;

o anti-Semites;

o LaRouche (See Note A.)

o John Birchers (Posse Comitatus 1970) (See Notes B and C.)

o Aryan Nations (a Christian Identity-linked racist org justifying its actions based on fear of the "decline of the white race" – Obama made these fears heighten);

o various apologists for Apartheid (including Nixon and Reagan)—of note because Apartheid was a Christian Nationalist/Racist Government (formal caste system) which had its own form of McCarthyism until 1992;

o Afrikaner pro-Apartheid groups (who have partnered with "White Power" groups in the US);

o Hardcore Christian Nationalists;

o Racist Right groups such as the Council of Conservative Citizens as well as more infamous groups like the Knights of the Ku Klux Klan;

o "Christian Patriot" Militias;

o Neoconservative Brothers-in-Arms;

o Christian Nation Promoters;

- And...finally Extreme Religious Cults (who can cause severe psychiatric injury including frank psychotic meltdowns and PTSD) including Scientology and the Unification Church (aka the Moonies).

LaRouche has been partnering with so-called "libertarians" linked with the Tea Party movement. This would be less of a Dominionist partnership and more of partnerships with the "racist right" -which LaRouche *has* been an active partner with other racist groups more definitively linked to Dominionism (*in this case, the "Christian Patriot" movements, the neo-Confederate secessionist movement--both of which are heavily Christian Reconstructionist--and Christian Identity, a documented sister-movement of the New Apostolic Reformation*).

As to Posse Comitatus and its links with the Birchers, this is more of a "right wing" alliance, but--of note--both groups have been closely tied together in regards to racist-right initiatives, and the direct descendants of the Posse Comitatus (*the numerous "Christian Patriot" militia groups*) and Birchers have been known to share partnerships even recently, especially with the rise of the "Tea Party" movement.

In particular, the linkage is probably closest with "Tenther" groups including the JBS; at least one "Tenther" group that has allied itself with the JBS explicitly calls for an identical model of governance and "leaderless resistance" to the Posse Comitatus

Several researchers, including Alex Bird, Chip Berlet, and especially Rachel Tabachnick have noted the increasing promotion of conspiracy theories popular in JBS and Posse Comitatus (and its descendants) in NAR and Christian Reconstructionist circles; this is in part because at least some NAR-linked leaders of the Dominionist movement are known to have connections.

Tim LaHaye, for instance--pretty much ultimately *the* founding father of the "religious right," even more so than Pat Robertson or Jerry Falwell--is known to be a member of the JBS and has mixed JBS conspiracy theory with preexisting conspiracy-theory narratives in NAR circles, and partly because of the cross-fertilization that has been occurring since the1970s onward between the racist-right and Dominionists as discussed in articles at www.talk2action.org.

The point of bringing all these names and groups forward is to demonstrate how for all their differences, they occasionally cross paths and that makes for formidable foes.

17 The God, Guns & Greed Club

"The most powerful conservative organization in America you've never heard of"

Who am I referring to? I'm talking about the scouts who comprised the whole "Palin-discovery" cruise to Alaska including William Kristol who wears several hats. He's a writer for the Weekly Standard to name one and a leader in the *Council for National Policy (CNP)* to name another.

Let's take a glance at the CNP. The first fact that should jump out as us, screaming, is that this secret cabal of Conservative Elitists was founded in 1981 by none other than Tim LeHaye, author of the book series *"Left Behind."* This wildly popular work of fiction tells a theatrical story about the End of Days, the Rapture and Armageddon. People die, cars crash, planes fall out of the sky as the "chosen" Christians (and that leaves out non-Born Agains and that means you, too Catholics) are sucked up into thin air and all that is left behind are their clothes. Yes, it's a grim picture: School bus drivers are sucked up and the bus loads of innocent children are killed. Plane pilots are poofed and the jet turns into a coffin in the sky.

These Dominionists absolutely love, love, *love* this stuff!! It scares the bejeezus out of their "sheeples" and keeps them firmly in the clutches of the Cult. Unbelievable.

And, as impossible as it seems, the author of this "Christian" science fiction is the founder of the group that makes seriously important decisions behind our backs in America.

This group is a remarkable collection of extremists where God, Guns & Greed all merge into one frightening think-tank on the outskirts of Washington, D.C. Apparently, those of us who are mere citizens of this country aren't important enough to be included in their backroom discussions about our fates in this country where they meet to discuss politics from a pulpit perspective. You can only play in their clubhouse if you are invited. Two years ago you could readily pull up their site and see the list of members. It has since been hidden from public view; even their members are warned not to share their membership list.

One of the research sites that follow the secretive goings on of the CNP is at seekgod.ca and they describe them in this way:

Many Evangelical, Pentecostal, Charismatic, Catholic, Mormon and other ecumenically-minded leaders are members of the Council for National Policy, the 500+ (varies per year) member organization which some suggest plans the strategy of the Religious Right and conservatives in the United States.

The CNP, according to their 1996 Telephone Directory, was founded in 1981. While those involved are from the United States, their organizations and influence cover the globe, both religiously and politically. Members include corporate executives, television evangelists, legislators, former military or high ranking government officers, leaders of "think tanks" dedicated to molding society and those who many view as Christian leadership. Members in many cases are owners or leaders from industry such as lumber, oil, mining, commodities, real estate, the media, including owners of radio, television and print, with all aspects of life covered. Many are involved in education, determining to influence society's direction by direct input with children and youth. Many advocate from the arena of right wing politics, conservatives, family friendly, reconstructionists, Dominionists, and so on.

CNP members are found in Christian organizations encompassing James Dobson's Focus on the Family, Bill Bright's Campus Crusade for Christ and it's many branches, Robert Weiner's Maranatha shepherding group, Gideons, Youth for Christ, World Vision, Wycliffe Bible Translators, Billy Graham Evangelical Assoc., Intercessors for America, International Charismatic Bible Ministries, National Evangelical Assoc., National Religious Broadcasters Assoc., Promise Keepers and many more. The potential spiritual impact of this organization, which claims educational status, could be unparalleled.

While many involved in the CNP have denied political activity in their respective organizations, the role of the CNP appears to be that of a policy and funding conduit for the Religious Right projects, both political and religious. Others would suggest they are merely a conservative group of individuals who get together to share ideas, network and hear "exciting speakers." Many non-Christians and deceived Christians would view many involved as representative of born-again Christians. However, one of the intents of the CNP seems to be that of appearing to be a mouthpiece of true Believers, which cannot be. Many are simply not Christian and others would make a claim, rather, to being conservative, holding 'traditional values' and family orientated. Many would also propagate the idea of transforming the United States back to its 'godly' heritage, to which there is no supporting Scripture." ~ seekgod.ca

You might think, "Damn! How can I see the list? Who's on it?" Well, there is this handy tool which allows us to "copy & paste" content on the web so that we can preserve it forever. My future book will include a more complete listing because their membership vacillates between 500 – 600 names. However, for now we will give you a very short list of the major players. The ones that we list here are tied directly to Dominionism.

Council for National Policy Board of Directors

(per 2008 Council for National Policy form 990 filed with the IRS)[20]:

Secretary Paul Weyrich (another longtime CNP member, founder of the Free Congress Foundation, has worked with the Heritage Foundation, and whom has run many, many front-groups of both orgs including groups proffering aid to the Contras under claims that said aid was meant for "missions" to (long-Christianized) indigenous peoples; works with members of Tradition, Family and Property (a neo-fascist group that idolizes the ultramontane-fascist regime of Francisco Franco) and is the primary "cat-herder" between neoconservative interests and Dominionists within the CNP);

Director Tony Perkins (head of the Family Research Council—one of only a few Dominionist groups to be listed as a hate group by Southern Poverty Law Center—and the Louisiana state affiliate of Focus on the Family (Louisiana Family Forum). Ringleader of the "Justice Sunday" and "Liberty Sunday" events[21]—illegal electioneering for pro-Dominionist Republican candidates that occurred in Southern Baptist churches and which were televised on "Godcasting" networks Trinity Broadcasting Network and Sky Angel (a Dominionist DSS company). Group started out as a Focus on the Family affiliate until FotF's tax-exempt was threatened; spun off into another independent org. The group—and Perkins— have close linkage to the "racist right"; _Perkins infamously paid David Duke (then head of the Knights of the Ku Klux Klan_, regarded as the most dangerous Klan group in the US due to its partnerships with neo-Nazis and racist militia groups) over $82,000 for a mailing list of KKK members for FRC direct marketing in 1996[22], and Perkins has also spoken before the Council of Conservative Citizens (the spiritual successor of the "White Citizen's Councils" infamous during the Civil Rights era).

Director Phyllis Schlafly (Founding member of CNP; Founder and head of the first political Dominionist group of the modern era, the Eagle Forum; her son, Andrew Schlafly, manages Conservapedia (promoted as a "conservative alternative" to the mainstream online encyclopedia Wikipedia). Probably most infamous for her role in scuttling the Equal Rights Amendment.)

Director Richard Viguerie (Founding member of CNP; founding member of Moral Majority (now defunct); best known for RAVCO direct-mailing empire which was first dedicated direct-mail campaign for the radical right (RAVCO started out with mailing lists borrowed from Young Americans for Freedom, a John Birch Society front-group, and Barry Goldwater's direct mail list);

Grover Norquist (may be on executive board as of 2009; longtime tax-protester, including "tax protester" group Americans for Tax Reform and a number of other "anti-tax" groups; on board of directors of National Rifle Association and American Conservative Union; best known for the quote "I don't want to abolish government. I simply want to reduce it to the size where I can drag it into the bathroom and drown it in the bathtub." Known co-author of Contract With America; became infamous for a racist statement re Barack Obama in which he compared the latter to "John Kerry with a tan." Has been a major promoter of the "Parental Rights Amendment,"[23] a proposed Constitutional amendment explicitly meant to strip child protection agencies of any jurisdiction in regards to child abuse (and particularly religiously motivated child abuse—a problem that is rife in Dominionist communities), promote a so-called "right" for parents to "discipline their children as they see fit" (including the use of "parent directed feeding" and "chastening rods" linked to *multiple* documented deaths of children in the US alone), and forbid the US from ratification of the Convention on the Rights of the Child (the US is the sole country in the *world* that is not a signatory and which has not given a commitment to ratify, almost entirely due to intensive political pressure from Dominionist groups that have promoted religiously motivated child abuse and educational neglect; even the provisional government of Somalia, the only other non-ratifying nation at present, has agreed to ratify it once the government has control over the whole of Somalia; in some countries, the Convention is effectively the only child abuse legislation in place and has been used very effectively to protect children)

My fellow researcher and contributor to this book, Alex Bird, pulled the above list and information from various public sources—this should give you an idea of how much the CNP is a "melting pot" of Dominionist and neoconservative interests.

Again, McCain allowed these scouts to sell him on Sarah Palin. Kristol, who is also Chairman of the Project for the New American Century, and who became enamored with her when he met Palin at the Governor's Mansion in Juneau went forth and gushed so overtly about her that his own conservative media pals had to say "enough about Palin!"

A blogger wrote at wonkette.com that,

"Kristol referred to her as "my heartthrob." And one blogger wrote, "They were her earliest cheerleaders, and I use that word because a friend of McCain's tells the New Yorker's Jane Mayer, "Kristol was out there shaking the pom-poms," for Palin as Vice Presidential nominee from early on."

18 Queen-Makers?

"...a former beauty-pageant contestant, and a real honey, too." – John Bolton, potential GOP presidential candidate

And from there Sarah Heath Palin was served up to McCain's handlers as the choice du jour. Nice! The guys fell in lust with her which is a stellar reason to promote her to a position second only to an elderly man that may or may not live through his four year term if elected president of the United States. Really smart bunch of fellas!

When you take into consideration the things said about her after the reconnaissance team went north to meet her, it is hard not to understand this in terms of the Stepford Wife meme that I talked about earlier in this book. The "Cruise-of-the-Conservative-Elites" was thoroughly written up in *The New Yorker* by Jane Mayer in 2007:

> On June 18, 2007, the first group disembarked in Juneau from the Holland America Line's M.S. Oosterdam, and went to the governor's mansion, a white wooden Colonial house with six two-story columns, for lunch. The contingent featured three of *The Weekly Standard's* top writers: William Kristol, the magazine's Washington-based editor, who is also an Op-Ed columnist for *the Times* and a regular commentator on "Fox News Sunday"; Fred Barnes, the magazine's executive editor and the co-host of "The Beltway Boys," a political talk show on Fox News; and Michael Gerson, the former

chief speechwriter for President Bush and a Washington Post columnist.

Now don't think that Palin was surprised by their arrival! Au contraire! Read this...

Palin was wooing a number of well-connected Washington conservative thinkers. In a stroke of luck, Palin did not have to go to the capital to meet these members of "the permanent political establishment"; they came to Alaska.

*Shortly after taking office, Palin received two memos from Paulette Simpson, the Alaska Federation of Republican Women leader, noting that two prominent conservative magazines— The Weekly Standard, **owned by Rupert Murdoch's News Corporation**, and National Review, founded by William F. Buckley, Jr.—were planning luxury cruises to Alaska in the summer of 2007, which would make stops in Juneau. Writers and editors from these publications had been enlisted to deliver lectures to politically minded vacationers. "The Governor was more than happy to meet these guys," Joe Balash, a special staff assistant to Palin, recalled.*

This is all so incestuous and insulting isn't it? They still act like this woman just emerged from nowhere, out of thin air, a fortuitous happenstance on the part of a few lucky conservatives innocently cruising through Alaska. NOT! Other trips were made to Alaska and Palin got herself up and high-tailed it to Juneau

in time to entertain at the Governor's Mansion that she seldom visited. One adoring visitor recalled Palin in high heels, [...] walking around this big Victorian house with rough Alaska floors ,saying, 'Hi, I'm Sarah.' She was 'striking,' he said. 'She has that aura that Clinton, Reagan, and Jack Kennedy had—magnetism that comes through much more strongly when you're in the same room.
- Jane Mayer, The New Yorker

First off, the spin began right there when they made up this fairy-tale portrayal of the Alaska Governor's mansion as though it were a rough-sawed log cabin in the wilderness. I have spent time in that mansion from my childhood through adulthood. I have personally known several of Alaska's governors and first ladies and have dined at the mansion on several occasions Though smaller than other governors homes in the United States, it is lovely, and has been refined, re-furbished and updated on more than one occasion.

This depiction ("rough Alaska floors") is a perfect example of the exaggerated, revisionist fiction that the Right uses at every turn in their telling of events. They began to package her as a commodity immediately and prepared to sell her as a chip off the ol' Reagan block. No requirement for reality here folks – it was all about the package. And, wow! Did it work for a frightened pool of conservatives watching the popularity of a young dynamic candidate named Barack Obama!

Bolton, [yes, John Bolton] for his part, was pleased that Palin, a hunting enthusiast, was familiar with his efforts to stave off international controls on the global flow of small weapons. She spoke knowledgeably about missile defense, too, he said, and discussed his role, in 2001, in guiding the Bush Administration's withdrawal from the Anti-Ballistic Missile Treaty.

Jay Nordlinger, a senior editor at National Review, had a more elemental response. In an online column, he described Palin as "a former beauty-pageant contestant, and a real honey, too. Am I allowed to say that? Probably not, but too bad."

According to several accounts, however, no connection made that day was more meaningful than the one struck between Palin and Dick Morris. "He had this very long conversation with her," Fowler recalled. Lowry laughed in remembering it: "The joke going around was that he was going to take credit for making her." (Nordlinger's column went on to say, "Her political career will probably take her beyond Alaska. Dick Morris is only one who thinks so.")

In fact, in an admiring column published in the Washington Post two days after Palin was chosen, Morris wrote:

> *"I will always remember taking her aside and telling her that she might one day be tapped to be Vice-President, given her record and the shortage of female political talent in the Republican Party. She will make one hell of a candidate, and hats off to McCain for picking her."* - The New Yorker, by Jane Mayer October 2008

Thus, the grooming and molding of Sarah Palin as a national candidate began.

A fellow neoconservative named Randy Scheunemann saw Palin for exactly what she is: a "blank slate." Bill Kristol had seen this movie before when he had to "brief" Dan Quayle as Bush, Sr.'s vice-presidential candidate; tutoring Palin on foreign affairs presented similar challenges. The fact that both Quayle and Palin hold such limited worldviews on most everything, let alone foreign affairs, political vultures and opportunists like Kristol & Co. see them as figures that they can mold. Meanwhile the rest of us see them as so dangerous and ill-prepared that we don't take them seriously, which is a great combination for these makers of political frankenmonsters.

So, when the time was right, Kristol & Co. moved in and dictated to the McCain campaign that Sarah Palin would be his running mate. Then, when the pick threatened to blow up in their faces, they allowed a debate to ensue that Palin's pick had been a knee-jerk reaction to target the female vote in America. Certainly, there actually are some women out there who would have voted for Palin because she was the same gender, but the majority of the population was not swayed because of this attribute. This was not the real attraction that simmered below the surface of this new-found "project" (as the McCain campaign referred to her) that would bring voters out in droves and support the McCain ticket - and the Republican Party strategists knew this very well.

She was chosen purposefully to ignite the Dominionists, but unfortunately the Republican "think tank" outsmarted themselves. She was too perfect, too malleable, and in the end, too divisive.

The masterminds, in their zealousness to usurp Barack Obama's spotlight the day after his acceptance speech at the Democratic National Convention, hastily chose a character based on the criteria that she was 1) female; and 2) a religious fanatic. There were no other litmus standards required for the appointment of Palin.

McCain made the conscious decision to forego not only what was honorable for him, but best for the country and the global community as well, by agreeing to put Palin on the ticket with him. He abandoned his principles and honor by selling his soul to the devil – or – as he called it "the agents of intolerance", remember?

His obsession made him as much a zealot as they are, in his quest for the White House. He got to the point where he was clearly willing to do anything to get there and at our expense. They used him, and it almost worked.

An Altar Call

"I'm like, OK, God, if there is an open door for me somewhere, this is what I always pray, I'm like, don't let me miss the open door. Show me where the open door is." ~ *Sarah Palin, on running for national office in the future, FOX News interview, Nov. 10, 2008*

Palin's devout religious views were an altar call resonating with conservative Christians across the country like a wildfire. Born-against raptured into the fold and onto the bandwagon! We see it happening again today, with all of these candidates today *all* vying for first in line.

Don't forget, in one of McCain's earlier attempts to call the White House his home, in his campaign of 2000, he made the fateful mistake of calling this cadre of extremists (known then as the Religious Right) "agents of intolerance." He never recovered from that. In fact, during much of his 2008 campaign, he continued to move away from this dedicated voting bloc by virtue of his close ties and overt dependency on Joe Lieberman. Lieberman, a former Democrat who changed his Party registration to Independent in 2007, pals around with Democrats and is an Orthodox Jew.

The possibility of McCain choosing Lieberman as his vice president loomed large and did not bode well for McCain's chances to garner the conservative Christian vote. This did not go unnoticed by the powers that manipulate the Republican Party. Thus, the courtship began and Palin had all the qualities they were seeking, not the least of which were her gaps in knowledge on foreign and domestic affairs. She was perfect for their agenda, (a real life "Manchurian Candidate") an individual who could be groomed to the Party to control the decisions, movements and outcomes of the office of the President of the United States. Those Sarah Palin is aligned with take the view that the ends absolutely justify the means.

They, *themselves*, sold her to us as a "maverick," a "rogue," and *they* don't know how to contain her? Palin went off-script from the very beginning causing quite the dilemma for these puppetmasters. She just wasn't supposed to be quite THAT mavericky and roguish! Now they are left in a quandary as they do political gymnastics deciding just what to do with this woman. They love her for the money she is raising and the crowds she is drawing out to vote Tea Party/Republican (TP/R), but they envy her for the attention she is getting, leaving some of them a little too far back in the shadows of her new found notoriety for their own ego-driven comfort level.

Palin's pseudo-celebrity status has grown far greater than what they had imagined. They have no choice now but to begrudgingly include her on some level because she has become a force in hardline conservative politics, whether they – or WE - like it or not. She has moved far beyond what their original needs were for her in 2008. They are experiencing that proverbial slap "upside the head" by their own hand (or, in much cruder parlance, they have "cock-blocked" themselves). What's that saying? Oh yeah: *"Be careful what you wish for."*

She lies silently like the "Don't Tread on Me" snake in the grass, after making an ass of herself in her statement about "blood libel" and other outrageous verbal regurgitations on the very day of the Memorial service for the Tucson victims. While we cannot be fooled into thinking that she is gone, her recent gaffes have been so egregious, that it could be she will finally fade into oblivion.

Enter the Change of Heart – The Bloom is off the Rose...

Or the "North Star" as she so humbly refers to herself. (This was her code name with the Secret Service.) Barely two years later and what a different story

Bill Kristol has to tell after his whirlwind love affair with Sarah Palin.

Crooks & Liars.com wrote this in 2011:

Bill Kristol went on MSNBC with Joe Scarborough. He did admit to be very disappointed in Sara Palin's performance after she quit being governor in Alaska and now is picking either Paul Ryan (WI) or Chris Christie (NJ) as his top choices to be the GOP's 2012 presidential candidate with Marco Rubio as VP. How the mighty Palin has fallen. Kristol was the man who touted her to John McCain and has been an avid Palin supporter ever since.

(rough transcript via MSNBC)

Q: Do you feel like you overestimated her and do you feel like she is fit to be a national Republican leader?

Kristol: I have a high regard for Sarah Palin, but I have to say I've been a little disappointed since she's resigned from governor. I thought she had a real chance to take the lead on real policy issues, to do a little more in terms of framing the policy agenda. I don't think she's particularly done, but she's shrewd, I wouldn't underestimate her.

Q: Has she lived up to the potential that you saw in Alaska?

Kristol: Maybe not quite, but she's young and she can do it in this campaign or she can do it four or eight years from now.

Kristol has always been enamored with Barbie Doll looking politicians since he was the chief of staff for Dan Quayle (He

*was called Quayle's Brain) and saw him as
the poster boy for Conservatives because of
his looks rather than substance, but as we
know he flamed out completely. That's why
Kristol fell in love with Sarah Palin on a
2007 cruise.*

*In June 2007, a cruise hosted by the
political journal The Weekly Standard set
anchor in Juneau, Alaska. Standard
editors William Kristol and Fred Barnes
then lunched with Governor Sarah Palin. It
was a moment of discovery [...]*

*The Daily Telegraph's Tim Shipman
saw this encounter as the launch of a
Neoconservative project surrounding
Palin. He interviewed a former Republican
White House official now at the American
Enterprise Institute about Palin: "She's
bright and she's a blank page. She's going
places and it's worth going there with her."
Asked if he sees her as a "project," the
former official said: "Your word, not mine,
but I wouldn't disagree with the sentiment.*

*Kristol can fairly lay claim to having
"discovered" Palin for Washington political
circles. Palin's name appeared in 41
Weekly Standard articles since the Juneau
meeting—starting with a paean entitled
"The Most Popular Governor" that ran
right after the reception.*

*He did help create a money making
Conservative personality in Palin that
attracts only the base of his party so he
failed again with his agenda. The polls all
tell the same story with her super high
negatives and that's why he's switched to
one of the youngsters of the Conservative
gibberish movement in Paul Ryan and a*

nasty debater in their new love, Chris Christie. - Crooks & Liars February 8, 2011

The circus never ends. If this doesn't tell you something about how it is all a game of deception and manipulation to attract the voters, nothing will. They played Russian-roulette with our lives, our country, and our futures, and all he can say is he is *"very disappointed in her performance???"*

If you have never taken all this seriously before, please take it seriously now. Do you see how they pull these mannequins out of the closet and sport them as qualified candidates? This is profoundly dangerous! It reaffirms my position that a *"Palin's America"* does not require Sarah Palin herself as the participant. We are looking at mannequin Ken coming rapidly at us in the person of Rick Perry.

A simple and literal adherence to Old Testament Christianity is bleeding into conservatism in America. Even if Palin has (finally) become a tabloid joke, there are others to move into her place. This is a version of Christianity that is unrecognizable to mainstream Christians, a bible-based sect that spans denominations and the continent. They successfully and thoroughly infested the Republican Party in the early 1990s and ran candidates in the Tea Party in 2010. They are embracing a broad spectrum of disenfranchised Americans who are being told who to "blame" in order to further the goals of religious and political conservative zealots in America. There is no time to waste, we must begin a national discussion about those taboo topics – POLITICS & RELIGION.

19 Onward Christian Soldiers?

*For they are demonic spirits. . . who go abroad
to the kings of the whole world, to assemble them for
battle on the great day of God the Almighty . . . at the
place which is called in Hebrew Armageddon . . .*
—Revelation 16:14,16

Now for something *really* scary! Our military is
awash with these extreme fundamentalist Dominionists. I
serve on the Executive Board of the Military Religious
Freedom Foundation alongside its founder, Michael L.
"Mikey" Weinstein and former U.S. Ambassador Joe
Wilson. Our whole purpose at MRFF is to represent the
needs of the over 22,000 (and growing) clients that we
have who are all members of our Armed Forces and 98%
of whom are mainstream Christians. They come to us
daily with the most horrific accounts of abuse of power in
their command by those who are Dominionist military
members forcing their version of radical Christianity on
them.

Our volunteers field hundreds and hundreds of
emails that are predominantly full of hate and anger
toward us because they cannot wrap their minds around
the fact that we are not anti-Christian, we are anti-
extremist. One of these dedicated volunteers put it very
succinctly,

> *"We can't fight Islamic belief run amok*
> *with Christian belief run amok."*

You can't say it much clearer than that.

Now, not to beat a deadhorse (so to speak) but
because the new extreme Right is so enamored with
attempting to usurp the Reagan image for themselves, it

becomes necessary to review some of what that really was, especially in terms of war and his Biblical worldview. For instance, it was his critics who began to consider whether the President's apparent belief in a particular biblical scenario for the end of the world meant that he might consider nuclear war a divine instrument.

Accordingly, more than one hundred religious figures, declared it *'profoundly disturbing"* that high *political leaders "might identify with extremists who believe that nuclear war is inevitable and imminent."* They also attacked the religious right for supposedly believing *"that reconciliation with America's adversaries is ultimately futile."* They cited eleven public and private utterances by Reagan on the possible imminence of Armageddon.

Because some Christians truly believe literal interpretations of the Bible and the tale of the end of the World, it is more than a little scary. This view flourishes in the U.S., not only in such sects as Jehovah's Witnesses and Herbert W. Armstrong's Worldwide Church of God but also within evangelical and fundamentalist Protestant churches. Literalists are called pre-millennialists because they believe Christ's Second Coming will precede an actual millennial kingdom (Revelation 20:6).

The most literal of the literalists are known as dispensationalists. They have devised elaborate systems of dividing history into divinely ordained eras. Reagan is among the millions influenced by this subculture, which is actively promoted by Bible colleges, seminaries, TV and radio preachers. Popular products of the Second Coming industry like Hal Lindsey's "The Late Great Planet Earth," which has an astonishing 15 million copies in print, is a good example of this.

Dispensationalists' versions of how these biblical prophecies will be fulfilled vary wildly and, to mainstream Protestants, seem forced and fanciful. Many contemporary "signs of the times" (famines, wars, earthquakes) have existed in almost all historical periods.

But the prophetic movement can point to the fulfillment of what they see as a major Biblical prediction. Two generations before Zionism emerged, dispensationalists insisted that one prologue to the End Times would be the return of the Jewish people to the Holy Land. Thus when Israel was founded in 1948, says Hal Lindsey, "the prophetic countdown began!" Israel's capture of Old Jerusalem in 1967 was equally portentous, since it seemed to fulfill Jesus' words in Luke 4:24 and made theoretically possible the rebuilding of the Temple on its original site, a long-established requirement of many dispensationalists. According to some, the Antichrist will make his headquarters there prior to Jesus' last coming.

Falwell's followers believe Christians will be swept or "raptured" into heaven before the great Tribulation. A common version of the end is that the Soviet Union (the evil northern empire of Ezekiel 38-39) will swoop down upon Israel but be defeated. After a later battle at Armageddon, God will inaugurate the millennium. This is so Tim LeHaye-like.

This is why it may seem confusing that so many Dominionists appear to talk out of both sides of their mouths when it comes to Judaism. The "love" Israel, and will, like Sarah Palin, even display Israeli flags (as she did in her office) or wear pins which combine the American flag/Israeli flag. Yet they often are so anti-Semitic! What you just read above gives you some insight as to why. It is about their perceived prophecies.

They must get the Jews rounded up and back home in order to hasten the Second Coming, and they don't want a two-state solution where Palestine would be organized as a separate entity. They need Israel to expand into Palestine so there is room for this forced pilgrimage that must take place.

In addition, here is the topper: They also have to re-build Solomon's Temple. There is one HUGE problem with that though; there is a structure in the way, and it is not just any structure. It is the second most revered holy structure in the Islamic religion, THE DOME OF OMAR!

And the problem is, the Dominionists take fulfilling this prophecy very, *very* literally.

God's Army, Cadets for Christ & USMC means U.S. Marines for Christ

It is growing ever more critical to understand the Dominionist need to take dominion over nations and the race to "harvest" as many souls as possible. Why? Because "signs" are popping everywhere they look. In Social-Psychology in college we studied the dynamics of "confirmation bias." It means just that: People will shut out anything contrary other than information that will confirm their pre-formulated bias. We see this everywhere nowadays on both the Right and the Left, but it is more exaggerated on the Right with the constant diet of fear and paranoia served in their politics and from their pulpits.

Nowhere is this more serious than in our Armed Forces. They are raptured in the story of the Four Horsemen of the Apocalypse, the foretelling of Armageddon as a fiery consumption of the earth, filled with tragic and horrific images.

This is being interpreted as an all-out nuclear holocaust. Bush, with his Gog and Magog rhetoric (see Chapter "The Chosen" for full Gog & Magog Bush quotes) was on his way there, and he looks like a moderate compared to these Dominionist hardliners like Perry, Palin, Bachmann & Co.

Remember the Seven Mountains prophecy by Loren Cunningham? Here is how he describes using our military personnel and federal tax dollars to disseminate the Bible:

> *I'm talking about those who are really being transformed, and they are endeavoring to transform in their realm.*

And I've seen it in government, I've seen it in the military, I've seen it in several ways.

Let me just mention the military. It was in a prayer meeting in 1971, or maybe 1972, I don't know, around there, in Switzerland, where God showed us to give away 100,000 Bibles among the V-Corp army of the military, US military in Germany. Well, we went, and I talked to Dr. Kenneth Taylor and he was coming through just for two hours in Germany, and I told him what had happened in the prayer meeting the day before, and he said, 'That's strange, I have 100,000 Bibles left over from a Billy Graham crusade. I'll give them to you, free, but you'll have to get the transportation.'

So I went to my friend, the chaplain, who was over the V-Corp army Colonel Lamberman, and he was over all the other chaplains, and I shared this vision with him, and he said, 'That's good. Tomorrow, I'm to meet with the generals. And I want you to give them the gospel, and then tell them what you want to do with the Bibles.'

So I did that the next day. And then they said, ok, we'll help you. If you can get the Navy and the Air Force to bring it over, we will get the green trucks to back up," [and if you consider 100,000 Bibles, these were big, thick Bibles, they will fill lots of trucks,] and they used the trucks to do it. And then the army, and the Navy and the Air Force, they brought them over, from Chicago, and we saw those distributed to the V-Corp army. At the funeral of my father, Colonel Lamberman and his wife were there, he said it was the greatest move of God he had ever seen: As the military guys were getting the Bible, and they were starting to apply it in their lives and we were praying and we were witnessing and we were working with them, they says they saw more people saved then [sic] any other time that we've seen—the power of the word.

And then his wife spoke up and she said, "You know, when we joined the military, we didn't know of any top military, generals or majors even, or even colonels that knew Jesus, and now it's full of them. And many of them were saved during that time of Bible distribution. I thought, "Oh, God just wants us to get his word out." ~ Loren Cunningham, YWAM[24]

"Not Christian Enough"

This is why we are alarmed everyday by the information that we receive at MRFF. As Mikey Weinstein says,

Either you stay quiet and let the evangelical chaplains shape a generation of the most powerful instrument of death (the U.S. Military) the world has ever known into an Army for Jesus, or you speak up. I couldn't stay quiet.

Basically what we are facing are Fundamentalist Dominionists that are – "preying" – not praying on non-fundamentalist Christians including in many respects other evangelical Christians

that are just not fundamentalist enough, telling them that,

'You may think you are Christian enough for us but you're not. And as a result you will burn eternally in the fires of Hell along with the Jews.'

And that's why I have got to be there to take the calls around the clock from our troops. Many times they will not give me their names, sometimes they will. I am her to report to you today that the Wall of Separation between Church & State in the military is nothing but smoke and debris. They are trying to turn our military into a faith-based initiative and that is not what our military is about.

To punctuate what he is saying here is a quote by Brigadier General Charles Duke, Jr. speaking at the United States Air Force Academy (USAFA), *"From the beginning we were a Godly Nation. We were conceived as a religious nation with freedom of religion but not free from God."*[25]

Mikey is a fighter who is driven beyond the limits of what is good for his own health but no one can stop him. He is a graduate of the USAFA; former JAG officer, and a former legal counsel in the Reagan White House. He worked as an attorney for Ross Perot in private business and believes passionately that the military is not in place to promote or defend any one's beliefs, rather the oath of our troops is to uphold the U.S. Constitution. He still considers himself a Republican of days gone by when it was a secular Party. His book is titled, *"With God On Our Side"* and his story is personal and shocking – a must read!

A final thought on this: In 2006 Rachel Grady and Heidi Ewing produced a movie titled, "Jesus Camp." This is the vacation Bible School for Dominionist children. A woman named Becky Fischer runs *"Kids in Ministry*

International" and puts on *"Kids on Fire School of Ministry"* located near Devil's Lake in North Dakota. (Interesting choice of location names). For those of you who have not yet seen this docufilm I encourage you to rent it. There are segments available to view on YouTube.

This is important to this part of the discussion because these children are being molded into little Dominionist jihadists where they are being prepared to lay down their lives in the name of Jesus. So, you take that training and indoctrination and add that to an all volunteer military at this point in our country and you have people enlisting every day, who truly believe that we are already in, not only a war, but a *holy* war, with Islam. At MRFF we are seeing the results of this daily and this should disturb all of us.

Over the past two years we have had victories stopping the engraving of Bible verses on our military rifle scopes by a subcontractor, who'd been working with the military for nearly forty years, located in Michigan named Trijicon. Military personnel contacted us to get these removed as they were being put further in harm's way when Muslims, both whom we were fighting and those we were training, took great offense to this religious war symbolism. Senior military officers were referring to them in the field as ".Jesus Rifles." We joined the voices of groups like Americans for the Separation of Church & State in protesting this blatant constitutional violation and it was ordered that they cease and desist as well as provide kits to scrub the engravings.

The founder of Trijicon, a professed Dominionist, ironically lost his life in a small plane accident when they flew into the side of a mountain in Alaska on a vacation. Name of that mountain? Gunsight Mountain.[26] I kid you not! I have seen it many, many times.

Another victory was in successfully petitioning the Pentagon to "un-invite" Franklin Graham, the Reverend Billy Graham's son, thereby stopping him from representing our nation on the National Day of Prayer in

2010. Graham is known to openly attack the entire Muslim population by saying that, "Islam is a wicked and evil religion." This is a dangerous message to broadcast from a national platform and does not represent the view of most Americans.

Another one of the more recent victories was getting a PowerPoint presentation pulled from the training class given to Missile Silo Officers and others at Vandenberg Air Force Base that used multiple Old Testament verses. This presentation attempted to instill a Biblical Christian justification for pushing the button that would end the world as we know it. This had been taught for nearly thirty years and the first time I saw the slides when Mikey sent them to me I was filled with fear, anger and stunned as a chill ran up my spine and tears welled in my eyes. This is not a game!

The Air Force is a primary target for conversion due to its air power and their interpretation of Revelation. Armageddon requires fire from the sky and the Air Force has the technology to fulfill that prophecy. *We must take this seriously!*

20 America in Black & White

"If Obama is elected will we still call it the White House?" ~heard by me within days of Obama's election

Yes, we are going to discuss racism. This has been brought up and slammed down numerous times since Barack Obama became a candidate in 2007 and increased radically once he was elected as President of the United States on November 4, 2008. It is an ugly side of humans, there is no argument there. And when topics this distasteful are brought up, it makes all of us uncomfortable. That includes those of us who would prefer to believe that discrimination based on skin color has faded in America. It also includes those of us in this country that are ashamed to admit that they may recognize this in themselves. No matter how we run from it, there is no denying that it exists.

So instead of trying not to talk about it, let's get it out on the table. In doing so we will all learn some pretty shocking information; I know I have. Coming from 1960s Alaska this was an even more distant concept to me, having only ever met one African American family during my childhood. Racism began to seep into my awareness when I visited relatives in Moberly, Missouri back in the 1970s. I didn't know these relatives well and quickly decided to keep it that way after hearing them refer in a degrading way to the African American population. I perceived them as Americans just like them, citizens of this country. To this day I physically wince at the sound of the "N" word – and that includes when I hear it used within the black community itself. It is degrading.

Here is some of the information that came out on the heels of Barack Obama becoming our 44th president of the United States. Elementary schoolchildren from Idaho, second and third graders, were chanting "Assassinate Obama!" on their school bus ride home. Black figures hung from nooses. Racial epithets were scrawled on homes and cars, and threats of violence against Americans just because of the color of their skin escalated.

Mark Potok, director of the Intelligence Project at the Southern Poverty Law Center, which monitors hate crimes states that there have been "hundreds" of incidents since the election. Potok, said he believes there is *"a large subset of white people in this country who feel that they are losing everything they know, that the country their forefathers built has somehow been stolen from them."*

Angela Glover Blackwell, founder of Policy link spoke about the air of racism since Obama was elected president:

> *Not only are we not post-racial, but Obama's election has either made race relations worse or brought out some lurking racism that we hadn't dealt with. 'It did become worst [sic] after we elected President Obama, wrote one commenter, identified as 'Granny,' 'That is when all the racism hidden and swept under the rug surfaced.*
>
> *I also agree that the election of an African American as President has unleashed a lot of racism,' wrote 'Idealist.' 'For example, I view much of the animosity within the Tea Party movement as being driven by racism, not principally by a concern over the size and role of government.'*

A letter came out addressed to the people of Coeur d'Alene, Idaho from Zach Beck. Beck is a known Aryan Nation leader and mentored under Richard Girnt Butler, the now deceased founder of the Church of Jesus Christ Christian in Idaho where he set up his compound on 20 acres in Hayden, Idaho. CJCC is an arm of Christian Identity. CI was founded on the belief that in the white race as the "true chosen people."

Adherents of Christian Identity claim that Europeans are the true descendants of the Biblical Jacob, making them the true people of Israel, and that it is those who are against the interests of European-descended Christians that are the true anti-Semites. This is a variation of "Serpent Seed" or two-seed theology that basically goes back even *further* than Jacob, in that they claim that white people are descendants of God (via Adam and Eve through Seth) while Semitic peoples (including persons of Jewish and Arab descent) are the literal sons of Satan via Cain.

In "Serpent Seed" mythos, Eve didn't just take the apple from the Serpent. She supposedly mated with the Serpent"

Two-seedline adherents believe that Jews are genetically compelled by their Satanic ancestry to carry on a conspiracy against the Adamic seedline and today have achieved almost complete control of the Earth through their illegitimate claim to the white race's status as God's chosen people. As a general rule, Christian Identity followers adhere to the traditional orthodox Christian views on the role of women, abortion, and homosexuality, and view racial miscegenation as a sin and a violation of God's laws as dictated in Genesis of 'kind after kind,' and that...

Since 1979, Aryan Nations has been engaged in prison outreach. This is an important aspect of the Aryan Nations' agenda, given that so many members of The Order and Aryan Nations are now serving long prison sentences. Aryan Nations corresponds on an ongoing basis with prison inmates through letters and the forwarding of its periodicals. In 1987, Aryan Nations began publishing a "prison outreach newsletter" called The Way, which has facilitated recruitment and connections between Aryan Nations and its offspring, Aryan Brotherhood, a network of prison gang members. In 2009, Aryan Nations Revival and Aryan Nations led by Pastor Jerald O'Brien merged, since both parties were ardent Christian Identity adherents.
- according to Wikipedia.

A disturbing trip to websites associated with these groups goes into these issues from their view. If you choose to visit, additional links to explore include the links to other Anglo-Saxon Christian ministries as well such as America's Promise Ministries (at www.amprom.org) located in Sand Point, Idaho a mere 40 miles from Hayden Lake. This area is a hotbed of Aryan and ultra-conservative-extreme Christian citizenry. It is also the birthplace of one Sarah Heath Palin who is warmly embraced there by extended family and friends on her frequent visits to her homeland.

The Assemblies of God church that Palin was raised in, indoctrinated in and whose theology she still subscribes, is in fact a grandmother church to the Christian Identity Movement.

An Associated Press article recently wrote:

Many have called the Tea Party movement racist or racially motivated. It's definitely a reaction against something. Was it coincidental that it collided with the election of America's first black president, or perhaps it is the expression of racial tension that we've been ignoring?

They quote a man who was born and raised in Georgia as saying, "I believe our nation is ruined and has been for several decades and the election of Obama is merely the culmination of the change. If you had real change it would involve all the members of (Obama's) church being deported," he said.

A southern school principal reportedly told a concerned parent about the racist backlash occurring in their area that, "Whether you like it or not, we're in the South, and there are a lot of people who are not happy with this decision."

That is not subtlety. That is overt racism and it is not meant as a joke. The only time people claim that they were just joking is when they get caught saying these horrible remarks. Rather handy isn't that. And no matter how hard people on all sides want to spin this, it is pure out and out racism that had a direct uprising due directly to the election of President Obama. The secret service told CNN within months after his inauguration that threats to our new president rose approximately four-fold! How can anyone ignore the racial component of what is happening in this country?

In the summer of 2009, this country saw the following:

- People attending town hall meetings in the summer of 2009 with weapons strapped to their hips claiming to be doing nothing more than exercising their Second Amendment rights;
- People claiming that it was and is simply an expression of free speech to portray

President Obama or his wife as a monkey, or a jungle native;
- People holding signs up calling President Obama a Muslim because he is half black and of African American descent.

To say that racism hasn't had a new awakening in America is just plain denial and ignorance. BJ Gallagher, a sociologist and co-author of the diversity book *A Peacock in the Land of Penguins* said:

> *If I can't hurt the person I'm angry at, then I'll vent my anger on a substitute, i.e., someone of the same race [that I am angry at].*
>
> *We saw the same thing happen after the 9-11 attacks, as a wave of anti-Muslim violence swept the country. We saw it happen after the Rodney King verdict, when Los Angeles blacks erupted in rage at the injustice perpetrated by "the white man." It's as stupid and ineffectual as kicking your dog when you've had a bad day at the office. But it happens a lot.*

Read Gallagher's a couple times over if you have to because this is truly the crux of the problem. The anger that we are now seeing was nowhere to be found during the Bush years as our country was taken further into economic disaster. Bush grew our federal government exponentially by hiring more people than ever before and creating more bureaucracy. He and his administration did more to remove our freedoms by eroding our privacies than any other president had and while all this was going on, *WHERE* were these angry conservatives!? If everything Bush did had done by a black Democratic president, one can't even imagine the outrage that would have ensued.

There is now considerable evidence that the very racism and anti-progressive movement that has exploded in the US is now being exported abroad. Anders Behring Breivik, a self-proclaimed "Conservative Christian" terrorist—(whom, as of this writing, is now linked to a terrorist bombing and mass murder that has taken the lives of 76 people, mostly children) conducted the terror operations as part of a claimed revival of the Knights Templar. (Ironically, the original Knights Templar were destroyed in part because of rumors of the worship of "Baphomet," likely a corruption of Mohammed; some writers have suspected the Knights Templar "went native" during the Crusades).

Analysis of Breivik's writings have shown he has been influenced heavily by hate-promoters in the US, including the use of specific phrases and comments that are hallmarks of Dominionist and racist-right groups here, phrasing *very* atypical of the traditional "racist right" of Norway, which is largely comprised of neo-Nazis and "Odinists"—people whom, much like Christian Identity, promote a racialist perversion of Norse neo-paganism.

In particular, he was a fan of Pam Gellar, a vociferously anti-Muslim writer (so vociferous that both she and her group Stop Islamization In America are considered hate promoters by SPLC) who has been especially active in promoting "birther" conspiracy theories that claim Barack Obama is not a native-born US citizen and is a crypto-Islamist. Breivik was a regular writer on a number of English and Norwegian hate forums including Jihad Watch (itself closely connected to Dominionism) and the Norwegian hate site Nordik.no, and apparently kept close links with anti-Muslim hate leaders in the "Tea Party" movement.

Specifically damning of his connections with American racists (in particular, those connected with the Dominionist movement) are several notes in Breivik's 1500-page manifesto *2083: A European Declaration of*

Independence. This includes more than a few comments that would slip past those not familiar with the history of Dominionist conspiracy theories.

Among other things, he extensively promotes a particular conspiracy theory popular in neopentecostal-Dominionist circles that dates back to the 50s that alleges that the UN (and worldwide Islamist movements) are in fact being secretly controlled by the Soviet Union in an effort to promote Marxism. The anti-UN "UN is a Soviet Plot" conspiracy theory started with Birchers, and combined with pre-existing conspiracy theories dating to the early versions of the Scofield Reference Bible claiming that Russia was the home of the Antichrist and would use Iran as a proxy to attack Israel). Starting on page 20 he promotes the concept of multiculturalism being a form of "Cultural Marxism," a term used by neoconservatives linked to the "racist right" (including, notably, Pat Buchanan and Andrew Breitbart) as a functional euphemism of the old "Secular Humanism" canard (where "secular humanists" and "cultural Marxists" are smear terms to "red-bait" or "atheist-bait" progressives and moderates). Throughout the manifesto, he uses images lifted almost verbatim from American sources on various "Tea Party" and racist forums.

There is even evidence in the manifesto he is being directly influenced by Dominionist hate groups in the US. On page 25 of the manifesto (in the middle of the rant about "cultural Marxism" and how modern European progressivism is apparently a Communist plot) he uses some distinct phrasing and capitalization of "Feminists and Homosexuals" that are the hallmark of a particular Dominionist hate group—the American Family Association, listed as a hate group in 2010 by SPLC . This listing was earned in part because of their promotion of Scott Lively, a Holocaust revisionist who has written a number of books essentially alleging the existence of a "gay cabal" that has caused the decline and destruction of empires since the time of Rome.

Breivik also did one other bit of "borrowing" from the AFA, reminiscent of how the AFA's OneNewsNow service often "borrows" material from AP feeds and replaces the word "gay" with "homosexual." (In one case this resulted in hilarity when the athlete Tyson Gay was referred to as "Tyson Homosexual" via said filter.) Part of the manifesto Breivik published is directly plagiarized from the "Unabomber Manifesto," with all occurrences of "leftists" changed to "cultural Marxist."

Other writings by Breivik also hint at more influence by Dominionist-linked "racist right" groups. Among other things, he speaks of "cultural Christianity" and "personal Christianity" in the manifesto—which plays not only with these concepts in "Christian Patriot" media, but also are reminiscent of how Dominionists will condemn mainstream Christianity as "lukewarm" and "church-centered" whereas the Dominionists describe themselves as "corporate Christianity."

A particularly favorite quotee is "Walid Shoebat," a person who alleges to have been an ex-PLO terrorist who converted to neopentecostal Christianity (the PLO were largely a secular group—not Islamist—and there is some considerable question as to the authenticity of his story on many different levels; more than one researcher has pointed out that this is an increasingly common "conversion trope" in Dominionist neopentecostal churches) and who is a regular on both anti-Muslim hate sites popular in the "Tea Party" movement *and* on the Dominionist "traveling pastor" circuit.[27]

This is not the only thing he's cribbed from American racist-right and Dominionist groups, however, and one final thing may be the most dangerous of all. In interviews with police (summarized on Aftenposten.no and other Norwegian and European news sites), he has indicated he managed two "revolutionary cells" and that upwards of eighty people may be involved in terrorist cells—organized *very* similarly to the concept of "leaderless resistance" in "Christian patriot" militias and to "termite cells" of the Army of God domestic terrorist network in the US (many of whom are encouraged to act alone as pseudo-"lone wolf" operations).

Even the violence, sadly, may have been inspired by Americans, and not just by the racialist and Dominionist terror cells in the US. We have actually had a similar terrorist attack in the US—thankfully of much lower scale than the Utøya Massacre, but still a horror nonetheless.

To me—along with the Oklahoma City Bombing—the incident most reminiscent of Breivik's killing spree is the Knoxville, Tennessee shooting at a Unitarian Universalist church on July 27, 2008. The killer in that case, Jim David Adkisson, was a major listener of right-wing hate radio and a follower of some of the very same sites as Breivik. He also had a manifesto specifically stating that the UU church had been targeted due to its progressivism and that he, too, wanted to start a revolt to "kill liberals." Like Breivik, Adkisson explicitly targeted a youth gathering, in this case, a performance of *Annie, Jr* performed by the youth of the congregation. Like Breivik, Adkisson explicitly cited anti-Muslim hate—claiming that "Democrats and Liberals" were "tying the hands of the government in the War on Terror."

The only difference? - the death toll - which is no comfort   at   all

21 How Do You Spell Tea Party? K-O-C-H

"There are some extremists there, but the rank and file are just normal people like us,"
David Koch of Koch Industries

A discussion about the formation of the Tea Party is necessary because of the dynamic they have brought into American conservative politics. I touched on how this newly recognized group of angry Americans even impacted and contributed to the terrorist mind of Norway's Breivik. They are doing the same with unstable and violent minds here as well. A huge part of their influence has been due to 24/7 coverage and support of their platforms through FOX Newscorp and its cadre of misinformed entertainers. But none of this would have seen the light of day if not for the billionaire brothers of Koch, Incorporated.

This is a tale about the men who put together a strategy to get the middle class, lower class, working people, blue-collar, middle American to drop their brains off on their way to get their talking points from the very machine that has destroyed our jobs, industries and infrastructure for decades.

These "just like" him people actually picked up a pitchfork and joined the rest of the villagers to protest the very benefits that they rely on – not the least of which are Social Security and Medicare.

"...He continued, *"And I admire them. It's probably the best **grassroots** uprising since 1776 in my opinion."*

Koch said this in his brief ThinkProgress interview after the swearing-in ceremony for House Speaker John Boehner (R-OH) that he was proud of the accomplishments of his front group Americans for Prosperity.

"You bet I am, man oh' man," he said. *"We're going to do more too in the next couple of years, you know."*[28]

The oil tycoon and his brother Charles have funneled money to fight for a host of right-wing, pro-business causes for the last three decades. Recently, they outspent Exxon Mobile on *"astroturf"* campaigns to misinform the American public about climate change legislation.

These statements are just a slice of a three part interview that Lee Fang of Think Progress.org did as a result of being in the right place at the right time. David Koch just *happened* to be in Washington, D.C. to witness his man Republican Representative of Ohio, John Boehner, be sworn in as the new Speaker of the House in January 2011. The outcome was an impromptu interview.

Think Progress is notably recognized as having been the most aggressive blog site pursuing the truths and facts around the influence of Koch Industries, owned by two brothers – David and Charles 74. David is the younger one at 68 who holds majority ownership and is currently estimated to be personally worth somewhere in the neighborhood of $21.5 BILLION. Combined with his brother's worth they tally a grand total of $35 BILLION.[29] These boys were handed a $300 million dollar fortune[30] from their father Fred Koch who among other things was one of the co-founders of the John Birch Society intending to "purify" America. That is chilling all by itself.

There are many terms used when discussing this whose meanings may not be fully understood. Some are repeated intentionally as a sort of "code." Here is a partial list.

"Grass root"

This term originated as a way to describe a spontaneous effort by citizens who organize informally, on their own, to either support or oppose political actions and/or candidates. Getting out the vote to support a particular candidate is a great example of local grass roots organizing. The key here is that a "grass roots movement" is not funded by outside monies; it is not organized by professional political consultants; it is genuinely an effort that epitomizes "community organizing." Something, by the way, the McCain/Palin campaign spent a lot of time yelling about as they criticized Barack Obama because – after all – he was nothing more [significant/worthy/qualified] than that of a "community organizer."

Interestingly enough, the use of the term grass roots is reported to have started with a 1903 news article about Theodore Roosevelt and running mate Eli Torrance. A Kansas political organizer was reported to say, *"Roosevelt and Torrance clubs will be organized in every locality. We will begin at the grass roots."* ~ Wikipedia

"Astroturfing"

This, sadly, is a term that I have grown very familiar with in the past couple of years directly related to my efforts to speak up and defend the separation of church and state in America. I am astroturfed daily! Here is what it means:

Unlike grass roots, this activity is totally organized and implemented by professionals, whether they be special interest groups, corporatists, political entities of opposing views and so on. They are made to seem like they are grass roots, as though it is just the outcry of the common man speaking up and exercising their First Amendment right to free speech.

This is not true! Don't let them snow you. In fact the term itself is coined intentionally to counter grass roots by referring to the fake grass mat of man-made astro turf. One term conjures the visual where one is authentic and each blade is individual, growing ever higher; the other never needs to be cut, holds its uniformity without question and remains firmly anchored in its place.

Now that we know that we understand these terms, let's talk about the Tea Party – shall we?

Isn't it interesting that one of the many companies owned by the Koch Bros. is Stainmaster Carpets? These guys are as artificial in their ability to identify with the typical American as their carpets are made of fine natural materials. Getting back to the opening quote of this segment by David Koch which definitely bears repeating,

"There are some extremists there, but most of the people are just normal rank and file people like us."[31]

REALLY? Just like you? Honestly, how can anyone in their right mind believe this stuff? (Like you, I find myself slipping into a false sense of security now and again by dismissing this as so outrageous, and so completely beyond comprehension that it just cannot possibly be a real threat. Then I am snapped back to reality with a jolt of panic because the sad, pathetic, inescapable truth of the matter is that people buy what they are selling!)

This guy knows that there are enough people in this country who are willing to do his bidding as long as he throws around the right key words – patriotism, anti-government, less regulation, less taxes, greenhouse gases are a myth, and the biggest crowd pleaser of all - God! Yes, the very same phraseology that we see used in the Dominionist circles as well.

Coincidence? Not for a minute.

The Koch Bros and thousands of other wealthy Americans have been at this game for a *very* long time. David Koch himself has eyed politics ambitiously and not only made a bid for the presidency in 1980, but he and/or his brother have created ultra-conservative forces such as the Cato Institute[32] (global warming deniers) and Citizens for the Environment [acid rain deniers and contains no actual "citizens"). They also funded Mercatus Center [33]which claimed that smog helps to prevent skin cancer!; Americans for Prosperity[34] (ah, we are getting closer); and none other than FreedomWorks. FreedomWorks is a story unto itself, founded, funded and fomented by David with the help of another "commoner," millionaire Steve Forbes[35] and former Congressman Dick Armey. And *that* my friends, is the story in a nutshell of how the Tea Party was birthed. Are you feeling the grass between your toes? Me neither...it is pretty messy in real life isn't it?

So after all those tries, all those groups, all that effort, *what* would it finally take for David Koch to really get a strangle-hold on how to control the Republican Party? What could have caused the shift in this country to lend itself to this breeding of a Party for extremists?

Enter our little conservative darling, wrapped in the flag, sleeping with her head on the Bible, and who enjoys fondling guns more than shooting them: Sarah Palin. Now, top her off with a half-white and half African American president. That spelled *pay dirt* for the likes of the Koch Bros! And, for those who even attempt to whitewash the racism with regard to Obama, save your breath, saying it isn't so does not change reality.

It took Palin's arrival into this dangerous mixture to take their efforts into the living rooms, (or kitchen tables as they always like to say). Suddenly, this huge demographic emerged of red and blue-blooded, Bible-believin', flag waving, gun-totin' angry Amuricans - at the ready.

They stumbled on a lethal combination of emotion, using fear and paranoia delivered by a package that was attractive to them. That in turn engaged factions in our country who were siphoned out of the bushes by Palin's rallying calls to action. It took these self-interested billionaires from being longtime Libertarians, to catapult their ideas into a newly formed coalescing of the social values voters, sovereign citizens and uber-conservative Christians – and voila! The formation of the Tea Party. How very "grass roots" of them!

When you have this kind of incalculable wealth, you can have your fingers in many pies, and they do. An article in the New Yorker by Jane Mayer titled, *"Covert Operations"* on August 30th, 2010 outlines very succinctly how their efforts are nothing less than an all out attack against President Obama. They have the wealth, therefore the power, to influence that outcome.

For instance, where have we heard that same goal stated recently and by whom? Oh yes! None other than Mr. Minority Leader himself, Republican Senator from Kentucky Addison "Mitch" McConnell made this brazen and arrogant pronouncement publicly in October 2011,

"The single most important thing we want to achieve is for President Obama to be a one-term president."[36]

Good thing they all have our best interests at heart, isn't it?

Against Their Own Best Interests

This all builds a crowd of motivated voters who are emotionally charged and who allow that emotion to blind them. This dynamic happens on both fringes of the right and the left, but this is more about the influence that creates an open door in the GOP that allows Dominionist candidates to walk through.

At a time where we have more access to information than at any other time in history, we actually know less. We are bombarded with information, and where once we had real investigative journalists and real news to turn to, now we have Infotainment and far too many sources from which to retrieve our information. Most of us are so busy with demands on our day-to-day lives that we don't even bother trying to get to the bottom of what is really going on in the world. We hear a sound bite that appeals to us, or we turn to a source recommended by friends, co-workers or church friends and never really dig in to the substance to determine what is fact or fiction. Suddenly we are making decisions that may be 100% against what is best for us and our families for generations.

We must actually wade through the rivers of marketing news now in order to discern what we really support, but all too often it comes down to attractiveness and appeal. Marketing, packaging and sales: the world of Infotainment

22 Igniting & Exciting Fear

"Stochastic terrorism is the use of mass communications to stir up random lone wolves to carry out violent or terrorist acts that are statistically predictable but individually unpredictable."

Sarah Palin's Camp Says Depraved Liberals Blame Sarah Palin for Mass Murders

Democratic Congresswoman Gabby Giffords was shot in the head along with 12 other victims (six of whom have died) on that fateful January day. The FBI has said Gabby was the target of the attack. Gabby was featured by name on Sarah Palin's target hit list, a list that was not only featured on her Facebook Page but also her SarahPac page as well. When this list was published, it was criticized violent suggestions, most notably in hindsight by Gabby Giffords, who said she feared it could lead to violence. Sarah Palin not only refused to take it down, but gloated over the controversy in speeches, tweets, and her Facebook Page.

After the tragic news of the mass shooting, Ms. Palin put out a brief statement in which she offered condolences and said she was praying for Gifford's family. Gee, that's nice, I thought, but where's the introspection? Where's the accountability? No, I don't think Sarah Palin is to blame for a crazy person shooting a Democratic representative who represented a government he thought was "treasonous." She didn't actually pull the trigger, after all. But she has deliberately and with malice aforethought helped to create and feed an atmosphere of hate, division, fear and paranoia, and an atmosphere of white nationalism that, according to law enforcement officials, it appears this young man embraced.

Such atmospheres are magnetic pulls for those prone to insanity. It's precisely for this reason that political leaders should not engage in violent rhetoric. Ms. Palin knows this. Ms. Palin was called out for inciting violence in Alaska. Ms. Palin was called out for inciting violence against then Senator Obama, his wife and children during the 2008 campaign season.

The attacks provoked a near lynch mob atmosphere at her rallies, with supporters yelling "terrorist" and "kill him" until the McCain campaign ordered her to tone down the rhetoric. But it has now emerged that her demagogic tone may have unintentionally encouraged white supremacists to go even further. The Secret Service warned the Obama family in mid October that they had seen a dramatic increase in the number of threats against the Democratic candidate, coinciding with Mrs. Palin's attacks."- Telegraph.co.uk

So, while Sarah Palin cannot be held *directly* accountable for the attack on Ms. Giffords, I do hold Sarah Palin accountable for irresponsible, selfish and cynical behavior. Ms. Palin has been aware of the consequences of her words for a long time now. Ms. Palin used to give out public statements as a governor that called for a "backlash" against "asinine" citizens who filed ethics complaints against her. Ms. Palin has seen the death threats her rabid, unstable "fans" have issued to anyone who dared to call Ms. Palin accountable, including Senator Yee of California whose only crime was to ask the university where Ms. Palin was speaking to disclose what it was paying her. For this, he received heinous death threats, faxes of a noose around his neck and President Obama's neck, and ugly, vile disgusting rhetoric dripping with gutter hate only fit for the mentally unstable. And those are Ms. Palin's "bestest" fans.

For those reasons, Ms. Palin is well aware of the consequences of her actions. Yet, instead of having had a re-think, Ms. Palin went to bed that night feeling like *she* was the victim there.

A nine year old girl was dead along with five other people, people with families, people who were someone's world, and yet Ms. Palin went to sleep last night feeling sorry for herself. This is where we have a disconnect that cannot pass.

The evening of the shooting, the Palin camp took to the airwaves to decry the unfair treatment Ms. Palin has received. The person who speaks for Ms. Palin and writes for her on Facebook gave an interview with conservative radio host Tammy Bruce wherein she decried that blaming Sarah Palin for the massacre was "obscene" and "appalling."

Her name is Rebecca Mansour and before being picked up by Palin to fill the void left by Meg Stapleton, (Palin's former press secretary who was thrown under the bus), Rebecca was one of the most vitriolic original contributors to a pro-Palin web site called "consesrvatives4palin.com" under the pen name "RAM." Her loyalty to Palin prompted her to move from her home in California and relocate to Fairbanks, Alaska in pursuit of recognition from Sarah.

She managed to weasel her way in at a time when Palin needed a new lackey, but I cannot imagine the frustration that RAM feels not truly being acknowledged for all that she does. She is intentionally down-played by Palin and hidden behind the curtains over at SarahPAC, even though she is the primary creator of the written word with Palin's name on it. It must be emasculating!

In fact, Rebecca Mansour went so far as to claim that the "target list" was not intended to allude to guns. Tammy Bruce's website introduces the interview thusly, *"Rebecca works for Governor Palin's SarahPAC and while she joins me personally and not on behalf of the PAC, she does address the shocking effort by depraved liberals to somehow blame Governor Palin for today's atrocity."* It's all about Sarah. (Oh, and demonizing the left as "depraved liberals" among other name calling.) Way to scale back the hate talk!

Ms. Mansour hasn't the faintest notion what she's talking about. In our country we have a culture of violence. Both sides have participated, but one side in particular has honed the rhetoric to a finely sharpened tool. What is so obscene and appalling is that instead of owning up to being a part of this culture of violence and *leading* this country in a moment of crisis, Ms. Palin is still trying to make this about *herself.*

Instead of praying about this horrible tragedy and having a "come to Jesus" moment wherein she faced up to her own responsibility here, Ms. Palin continues to try to grab the spotlight. This is really about "me," she shouts. This is about how I'm picked on. It's not about the obscene deaths of six other people or a country of grieving Americans who are frightened to disagree with their neighbors about politics.

Recall if you will the Tennessee man whose car was rammed over his Obama bumper sticker shortly after Ms. Palin urged her supporters, *"That bumper sticker that maybe you'll see on the next Subaru driving by — an Obama bumper sticker — you should stop the driver and say, 'So how is that hopey, changey thing working out for ya?'"* That man had his young daughter in his car when his vehicle was rammed repeatedly by an enraged driver. In court affidavits, the bumper sticker is mentioned as the reason for the road rage:

> *On 3-25-10 Harry Weisiger pulled up behind Mark Duren's Toyota Camry at a stop sign. He blew his horn at Duren to get his attention. He then began to point at Duren's OBAMA/BIDEN bumper sticker.*

217

He then began to stick up the middle finger of both of his hands to Duren. When Duren left the stop sign, Weisiger rushed up to him and began to bump his vehicle into Duren's Camry. Weisiger then used his Vehicle to push Duren's Camry into a driveway located at 2539 Blair Blvd. There was proprety (sic) damage to both vehicles and Defendant left the scene without stopping.

Instead of owning up to how she has targeted liberals, the Palin camp has chosen to feel victimized. And while Mansour goes out of her way to say she's not Ms. Palin's spokesperson, the culture of victimization that Ms. Palin has been carefully tending in her hothouse of self pity until its spores invade even the most immune environments (cries of the press invading her "privacy" even as she is *shooting her reality show*) has been impossible to miss these past two years. Mansour's proliferation of outrage is pure Palin.

As for the offensive claim that the graphics weren't intended to indicate guns, Ms. Palin refuted that notion herself through various tweets and speeches. Here's Ms. Palin's Facebook response to the outcry against her graphics:

"In the battle, set your sights on next season's targets! From the shot across the bow – the first second's tip-off – your leaders will be in the enemy's crosshairs, so you must execute strong defensive tactics. You won't win only playing defense, so get on offense! The crossfire is intense, so penetrate through enemy territory by bombing through the press, and use your strong weapons – your Big Guns – to drive to the hole. Shoot with accuracy; aim high

and remember it takes blood, sweat and tears to win.

Focus on the goal and fight for it. If the gate is closed, go over the fence. If the fence is too high, pole vault in. If that doesn't work, parachute in. If the other side tries to push back, your attitude should be "go for it." Get in their faces and argue with them. Every possession is a battle; you'll only win the war if you've picked your battles wisely. No matter how tough it gets, never retreat, instead RELOAD!"

If that isn't enough, you can Google gun sight graphics. But honestly, who in their right mind would even make this argument? Ms. Palin knows the power of imagery and symbols. This is how the Right has been winning the battle of "fear over thought" for quite some time now. This pathetic, absurd attempt to distance themselves from reality and from their own responsibility doesn't merit any response by reasonable people.

Ms. Palin and her fans have taken refuge in the fact that other politicians have made violent metaphors. This is true. However, Ms. Palin is among the Hateful Gang of Four who have consistently, with deliberative purpose, and in fact without relent, cynically used the division in this country to further their own means. Ms. Palin has a pattern of using violent rhetoric. Ms. Palin never "retreats," she "reloads." Ms. Palin takes offense when it's suggested that she walk it back a tad. But more importantly, a Democratic Congresswoman suffered an assassination attempt and thus, the attempts at modern day false equivalency are barren of lucidity.

I'm hard pressed to think of a politician who has so consistently beaten the drum of violence as Ms. Palin. It is, in fact, why a good many Americans did not vote for her in 2008. This is what drove them away from their base camp of the Republican Party. They could not partake in the hate. Many of them sat it out while others voted for President Obama, even though they didn't agree with his politics.

This says good things about Americans. While we are a nation divided in many ways, while we are at a low point in history right now, in our souls, Americans are always reaching for the higher point. Americans do get pulled away from the issues and distracted by the Paris Hiltons of the world, we are greedy and prone to consumerism and self-absorbed at times. However, in times of crisis, when it really matters, Americans band together and the fighting spirit of a nation of immigrants comes together to take a stand for liberty, for freedom, for equality, and for justice. We have many faults, but we have brave spirits whose hearts see past the noxious fumes of disguise and demagoguery. Americans said no to hate in 2008. And we will do so again.

Our liberty is at stake. Our democratic process is at stake. Our freedom of speech is at stake. Because freedom of speech doesn't just cover the haters who screech violence against their opposition and then cover their behinds after the fact in cowardice. No, freedom of speech covers you and me as well. We have a right to have our voices heard in the wilderness without feeling terrorized. To those who continue to speak out even as they are threatened and their families threatened with violence by an out of control, extremist, angry contingency being urged on from the sidelines by yellow-bellied, morally devoid cowards, I salute you.

This isn't about Sarah Palin, even though she thinks it is. It's about America. This is our moment to seize the good in us and take a united stand for freedom and democracy. Don't be cowed by the outcries of victimization by the right. We are all grownups here, except for Christina Taylor Green, who will never be given the chance to grow up now.

Enough.

Palin Hit List Shows Pattern of Successful Targeting for Terror

Palin's hit list involved 20 Democrats who voted yes for healthcare. The Republicans ran on repealing healthcare in the 2010 elections. The Republicans also spent the last two years rabble rousing over healthcare reform.

The legal definition of terrorism is: "Terrorist involves the systematic use of terror or violence to achieve political goals. The targets of terrorism include government officials, identified individuals or groups, and innocent bystanders." Terrorism involves acts by subversives, acts of annihilation, criminal acts, demolition, destruction, extermination, fanaticism, revolution, terrorist act, or tyranny.

The political goal of the Republicans is to keep the Obama administration from reversing the last 20 years of loose oversight over corporations. In order to accomplish this, the Koch brothers funded the Tea Party and set their foot soldiers into motion. Obstructing healthcare reform was their first goal and the Koch brothers would tell you that this is because they are free market liberty ideologues. (Ironically, healthcare reform uses free market principle of competition among private entities to achieve its goal but it also involves stronger regulations and this is what the corporatists feel they must fight).

Historically, ideology has motivated Middle Eastern terrorist regimes, where religious fundamentalism is now combined with secular opposition as a source of violence. This sounds frighteningly like the merger of the hard Dominionist fundamentalist Christians (Palin) with the far right Tea Party. An important psychological component of terrorism is the symbolism behind it, and hence the targets of terrorism are symbols of the state (your elected representatives) or of social norms. Thorton defined terrorism thusly: "In an internal war situation, terror is a symbolic act designed to influence political behavior by extra-normal means, entailing the use or threat of violence."

And that's the real point – the threat of violence is enough because terrorism works on the psychology of the targets. It's a form of extreme political behavior and its effectiveness in influencing political events depends on arousing emotions. Does this sound familiar? Recall the fear of the town hall meetings, the outrage when the average citizen couldn't be heard, the outrage over Palin's hit list, Bachmann's call to raise arms against this government and Angle's second amendment remedies. Recall how we adopted to this behavior, subtly adjusting our expectations and reactions so as not to provoke the beast. In order for political terrorism to be successful, the target audience must feel psychologically threatened.

The target audience here would be the majority of Americans and our elected officials. This is why, as we try to hold these folks accountable for their actions, we're getting nothing but push back, further fanaticism and deliberate invoking of our outrage with their staunch denials of responsibility. They know how to control the reaction. If they keep mounting and escalating their offense, it will keep us hopping from one crisis to the next without our ever being able to adequately deal with any of them. This is a common tactic used by anyone employing psychological terror in order to effect control.

Terrorism requires more than the lone gunman. Effective political terrorism involves leaders and a network of supporters. Studies show that leaders of terrorists regimes are often what we refer to as the narcissistic personality type, people with the charisma to make violent behavior seem attractive and who fail to take or feel responsibility for their actions. This can combine with what is termed neurotic hostility, which involves sensitivity to criticism and a deeply suspicious, aggressive nature.

The network of supporters takes on the tasks of public relations, fund raising, and propaganda in addition to the actual perpetrators of the violence. It could be suggested that the Republican Party leaders mounted the public relations campaign against healthcare reform using violent rhetoric and inaccurate characterizations of the bill (with the larger target being to disrupt and disempower the Obama administration), funded by the Koch brothers who propped up the Tea Party foot soldiers "grass roots movement." All the while, Fox News provided the propaganda necessary to form the complete network in order to create the climate for political terrorism.

A perfect example of this would be the successful systemic disruption of town hall meetings by Tea Party foot soldiers, which resulted in the political goal of creating chaos and fear. Lawmakers were afraid to vote for it and citizens were afraid to go speak to their representatives. While healthcare miraculously got passed even after months of political threats and violence, a part of the terrorist's mission was accomplished. The lawmakers were now afraid of the Tea Party. Note that the mainline media was complicit in this effort as it took the media a long time to begin to identify that perhaps the Tea Party was not a grassroots movement of angry people but rather a well-funded astroturfed missile aimed at healthcare reform by financial interests.

Many who've studied the motives behind those who enact the actual act of violence suggest that to assume the individual terrorist is mentally ill is to ignore the political and social issues raised by terrorism. Rather than mere mental illness driving terrorists, psychologists find that terrorism is more likely to be a product of frustrated but rational idealism. However, the perpetrator of the actual violence need not subscribe to the political agenda of the organization.

Rather, Fred Kaplan suggests that the actual terrorists (rather than the organization behind them) are driven by feelings of inferiority and impotence stemming from the natural self-righteousness inherent within the terrorist mindset. However, studies also show that far right terrorist groups employ the insanity defense more often than far left terrorists groups, as indeed, far right terrorists (who may have been attracted to the glorification of violence typical of right wing terrorism which would tend to attract the more deeply disturbed) display a far higher incidence of psychotic personalities than do their left wing counterparts.

Any effective terrorist campaign must use the threat of violence, even if discrete, in order to achieve its goal. As it pertains to the effectiveness of Sarah Palin's hit list (i.e., those targeted by the "leader" and those who were then threatened by the random foot soldiers in what is being called "stochastic terrorism"), at least 11 of the 20 representatives on Palin's hit list received death threats (and one suffered an assassination attempt) after being placed in Palin's crosshairs (most of them immediately after the list came out). That is a successful terrorism campaign, reaching over 50% of its intended targets plus the added impact of terrifying those who witnessed or just heard about the massacre.

One of the intended consequences of terrorism is to leave the audience too emotionally vulnerable and exhausted to react to the next attack, which most likely will be an attempt to get whatever the terrorist organization wants from the audience. This is also referred to as bargaining, but of course, it's not really bargaining when the power remains with the terrorist organization precisely because they hit the audience when it's been weakened and distracted by grief, horror, or fear.

Here's Palin from earlier this year when giving a speech to the Tea Party, mocking the concern shown over her map with the crosshairs on Democrats across the country, "This B.S. coming from the lamestream media lately about us inciting violence, don't let the conversation be subverted, don't let a conversation like that get you off track." Yes, by all means, stay on track, er target.

Imagine if it were Islamic anti-government radicals who had been spreading the sort of lies and propaganda the GOP has when this brutal massacre occurred. How would the nation react to their attempts to distance themselves from their own words and graphics? How would the media and the American people respond to the rage of Sarah Palin, if she were dressed as fundamentalist Muslim?

Interestingly, people who are psychotic are not inherently violent toward others; however substance abuse significantly raises the rate of violence in people with schizophrenia — but also in people who do not have any mental illness. So how does this play into the notion that these psychotic madmen go around shooting people but are not influenced by their culture? It doesn't.

A specific form of psychosis is schizophrenia, though it should be noted that labels such as schizophrenia are utilized for diagnostic purposes and often over-used when they become the mental illness du jour; still the symptoms are real and hence the label of the illness is simply a way to distinguish the symptoms from other mental illnesses.

Positive Symptoms of Schizophrenia:

Delusions are firmly held erroneous beliefs due to distortions or exaggerations of reasoning and/or misinterpretations of perceptions or experiences. Delusions of being followed or watched are common, as are beliefs that comments, radio or TV programs, etc., are directing special messages directly to him/her.

To suggest that delusions are things that are not a part of our culture suggests that the belief is at odds with reality – but sadly, in our case, Glenn Beck is allowed to preach delusions to his audience every day. He preaches demonstrably false delusions about progressives being violent and out to get the Right, about the government coming to take all of his audience's freedoms away, about currency, about Obama being like Hitler, and more. Palin, Beck, Limbaugh and in fact much of Fox News (the Gang of Four) regularly implement rhetoric such as 'socialism' and 'communism' — dog whistle language for white supremacists about Jews and "others" taking over the country. None of these things has a basis in reality and as such, is not opinion but delusion.

Allowing Glenn Beck to sell his delusions as reality every day on Fox News mainlines these ideas until they are a seemingly legitimate belief system in a certain subset of the culture. How then can the Right claim Loughner is a madman when he believes many of the things Beck preaches, whether or not he ever listened to Glenn Beck?

Glenn Beck hardly exists in a vacuum. His words get repeated, his beliefs seep into the broader culture often unchallenged – and so what we have in effect is a subset of people who would have one of the largest symptoms of psychosis because they believe things that are themselves demonstrably false. At this point, his rhetoric has become dangerous.

Now, among this subset of people who believe Glenn Beck is telling them the truth, or who hear of his ideas as they permeate the culture at large and to whom they ring somewhat true or for whom the ideas feed an already existing paranoia and subsequent break with reality, we have waiting in the dark someone who is suffering from the number one symptom of psychosis – that is, he believes the people on TV and the radio are talking to him and have a secret message just for him, like Beck telling his audience to just "shoot them."

Although sadly, Beck achieved his mission long before that direct statement – for he is constantly warning his audience about how progressives, liberals and Obama are coming for them. He is the match to the psychotic's already existing paranoia and he or Sarah Palin is also then the special message.

If you pair that symptom up with the wide-spread pollution of paranoia carefully tended to by Beck et al, a dangerous marriage of psychosis with a carefully aimed persecution complex combine to form the special message for the already psychotic.

Glenn Beck has created a subset of people who are now broken from reality – these are people with whom their family can no longer discuss politics because they are not operating within the confines of this culture. They are in their own special group, a culture defined by paranoia and a belief that everyone else is lying to them. Within this group, or even on the fringes of this group, are people who are already not mentally fit. They are ripe pickings for the paranoia Beck sells.

So whether a person like the liberal church shooter read Beck (he did) and was a fan of Palin (he was), or the Tides shooter listened to Beck (he did), the Holocaust Museum shooter who was a huge Palin fan, birther, Pat Buchannan reader who parroted Palin's 2008 campaign lines about "media deception" (he did) or the Pittsburgh cop killer had just uploaded a Beck video (he had), or perhaps just heard Beck in their living room every night in the background or perhaps their father was a Beck fan and railed about Beck's paranoid beliefs over the dinner table or perhaps he overheard others repeating Beck's distortions of reality over the water cooler at work – he need not have a direct connection to Beck in order to be influenced by Beck's deliberate breeding of psychosis as defined by a break with reality. The use of mass communication to inspire a random, mentally unbalanced person to commit an act of terrorism has a name; it's called stochastic terrorism.

In all of these ways, claims. that because the shooter was a "madman" exonerate Glenn Beck and Sarah Palin are exceptionally disingenuous. Beck and

Palin speak to the already at risk, stoking the paranoia and fear each and every day, deliberately and with malice. They are actually breeding armies of mentally disturbed people who are no longer in touch with reality. This is very dangerous. Then, with words about "taking them out", graphics with crosshairs showing who the enemy is, and relentless messages of imminent danger at the hands of these enemies, Beck and Palin et al have lit the match under the already psychotic and in some cases, actually caused the break with reality that brought about the psychosis.

It's completely dishonest to suggest that Beck and Palin exist in a vacuum wherein their words never reach the mentally ill. Their words have seeped into the culture such that Palin's malapropism "refudiate" was made a new word in the Oxford dictionary. Death Panels became a national talking point.

Beck and Palin's words do matter, they have taken root in the culture, and as such, they have created a subset of people who are not dealing with reality. When you add their violent, irresponsible rhetoric to this mix, you will eventually get violence by their foot soldiers.

It is inevitable, it is predictable, and it is reprehensible.

Even knowing this might be the case, a normal person would cut down on their rhetoric. But what we have here are two leaders so cynical, so disturbed themselves, so narcissistic and so power hungry that they will not back down regardless of the consequences. Things are so bad now that the British want Rupert Murdoch to answer for Glenn Beck and the Australians are warning that they will charge Palin with incitement to violence if she ever steps foot in their country.

Meanwhile, in this country, we are busy playing nice with the angry Right wing – no one wants to hurt their feelings by pointing out reality. We must all adopt the absolute crap line that this was a lone gunman. Like all the other oddly Right wing lone gunmen who believed the paranoid things they hear on Fox News.

Silence is complicity and the truth might be ugly but it's still the truth. Our media has become the overwhelmed babysitter, favoring the loudest complainer and bribing the instigator with sugar — an irresponsible, short-term solution to quell the wailing. Our culture is eroding by the very political correctness of false equivalency and pseudo niceness the right pretends to abhor but never fails to take advantage of.

It isn't that if Glenn Beck and Sarah Palin walk it back there will be no more insane shooters. But without access to the paranoia, without access to leaders who confirm the paranoia and direct the rage and fear, the distance between psychosis and psychotic action could be much   larger.

The number one symptom of psychosis is believing that people on the TV and radio have a special message for the psychotic. Given this fact, how can anyone suggest that a shooter exposed to this kind of paranoia on a daily basis was not influenced by it? And even more dangerously, how can anyone deny that we have an entire subset of the culture who actually believe what the Gang of Four sell, meaning that they are all suffering from delusions – breaks with reality.

When the next shooter goes off, having spewed the exact right wing, white supremacist, and anti-government paranoia as repeatedly sold by Sarah Palin, Glenn Beck and the Gang of Four, must we be sure to immediately protect those who will be blamed? Is it more important that they not be held falsely accountable or get their feelings hurt than that we have a civil society that operates in reality? The fact that we, as reflected by the mainline media, have chosen to value Sarah Palin and Glenn Beck's feelings over reality and over a civilized society is distressing and alarming. No one is suggesting that they pulled the trigger. But their incendiary rhetoric is a contributing factor and this cannot be denied.

Leah L. Burton

Just how many more lone gunman — "bad apples" — would you say they have left in their deliberately created culture of the delusional?

23 "Time & Triggers" Love Letters from "Christian Patriots"

..."*I love Jesus, and the cross and if you don't,
I hope someone rapes you."* ~ *from FOX Facebook*

The hate and threats of violence are vile and it is offensive that these cretins call themselves Christians! The more successful I am in getting my message out, the more the hate ratchets up another notch.

They have spelled it out for me by telling me that I am, *"a 'tool' and will suffer torture before death."* In contrast, the, *"leaders of this movement to 'expunge Christianity from America' will die quickly."* (Guess I had better elevate myself to a "leader" status to avoid the torture!) One guy told me that they *"are almost ready"* in one of many long emails laying it all out for me. I am including the entire email – misspellings and all - in order to maintain authenticity. This one came in Spring 2011...

Leah,

But you must know and fully understand, WE THE PEOPLE are not going far, nor for long. WE THE PEOPLE are organizing, preparing and we are going to stand. Time & triggers will dictate that and the radicals pushing there agendas will bring it more quickly.

Lets see what happens when we are attacked again thru these radical progressives reckless complacency, or thru our open borders the progressives wont close or control.

Lets see what happens when another Muslim 'Islam', goes off and kills another company of good American Soldiers or worse. Lets see what happens when we get those sick screaming Allah homocide bombers in our malls, in a school or explode an entire city or state.

Lets see what happens when the Illegal drug lord and friends take control of a border town or worse.

These beasts and their hell are already here and more are coming by deception and distractions and because of the progressives radical ideology!! Many of us Americans feel that it is organizations like yours and other well know enemies alike from within, that is helping America to fall and quickly.

And with a current radical & co in the white house and the liberal stinch on our hill. This ilk is taking full advantage of the American people. America has woken up tho and in a way she hasn't in 232 years. Time & triggers will save her and our Christian Constitution. God I pray. Or there is going to be one hell of a purge trying to save her and all WE THE PEOPLE are and have been. Who will be purged is known only to God. Our Chrisitan God. Because many are praying for it and many will pay for it as well.

Americans are funny that way and WE THE PEOPLE are angry beyond belief. A global peace loving people. It is just a matter of time & triggers. I am only a single American speaking the truth to you of what is really happening in America. This is no secret sir.

Leah, I do understand and appreciate what you are saying. I'm just so sick and done with the ACLU, La Raza and several other groups with radical progressive agendas telling Americans we can't openly defend or display OUR values, beliefs and traditions. Especially if they are Christian or Jewish. Too many others 'legally & ilegally' have entered our country only to try and 'change it' to be like theirs or worse. They demand and expect entitlements they have NOT earned or contributed too.

I will not turn the other cheek anymore and millions of other Americans are not going to either my friend. These progressive despots and   traitors are reckless and arrogant in changing US as quickly as they can. These despots don't want to close our borders or even control who is coming across them. These despots do not recognize our countries laws legally or morally either. Or they wouldnt demand changing them and forcing the MAJORITY of Americans to change.

You call it preserving & defending too. Or to be PC. You interpret, reinterpret and manipulate WE THE PEOPLES Constitution to be all inclusive, inviting and accepting of any and all indifferences and all immoralities.

Christian Moral law reinterpreted by Satan and his demons. Only Satan and his ilk would attack such valuable American values and traditions.

I have been conceding my Christian rights and values for 50 years. I have played nicely with my brethren. I DO mind, when people 'don't want' to assimilate and become American!! They do not accept, respect or appreciate our rich Christian culture and the Christian Foundation America WAS built upon. It wasnt Allahs, Buddas or Harrys!. It was Americas is the exact same culture as Israels was built upon!! A God of Christianity and the Lord RULES over our land!! That is the progressive radicals problem sir.

Don't tell us we have to bend to all of your customs and traditions or even compromise or concede anymore of ours to accomidate them, and dont tell us to take OURS down or hide them either. (I'm not saying your meaning you personally). Pretty simple ha.

Dont expect me to conform or even except this satanic behavior or rule of PC law in America. Your fight or your agenda grows and WE THE PEOPLE are preparing. It is only a matter of time before WE THE PEOPLE collide.

WE THE PEOPLE of these United States are very much on to the educated cultural elite progressives and radicals invading and deeply rooted. **We are preparing to revolt and it isn't far off my friend.** Many innocent will get caught unprepared and off guard. Many innocent will be caught in the way. The progressives will be at fault. It will be them to blame Americans 'WE THE PEOPLE', have had enough.

Our troops are fighting for 'America', and to me and millions of Patriot Americans and our children........we are not *a Muslim country and we will NEVER be. I applaud your opinion......as well, you should applaud mine and the millions and millions in majority. It's called "Freedom of SPEECH", it is MY 1st amendment right.*

I still have MY 2nd amendment rights to back the 1st up. WE THE PEOPLE are storing away iron & brass like never before. Your movement dont know America or your movement is reckless & blind to reality in denial.

As you continue forward with your radical 'change' agenda. Real change is coming. So you call me and my fellow Americans a racist, hypocrite, bigot or whatever other slanerous word you would like to call me, and these other patriots. As Americans, we have been called alot worse here and abroad. I can take it. I know the truth and I am a PROUD American.

Please send this on to Jay Sharlet at Rolling Stone Magazine or any other you would like. I stand by my words as a American patriot, veteran and Christian. I will stand against all domestic tyranny when WE THE PEOPLE finally stand.

I am a Oath Keeper and I am a true American Minuteman.

I also have more for them to add to the story. I might even share the patriot movement I am speaking of on the web. Thank you and good day and good bye.......

Mike Price/III

Okay, then! As I say - this is only one example. And for anyone out there who is ready to jump on me and say that I am unfairly connecting these folks to the Perry, Palin, Bachmann & Co. wagon – let me share a bit more....

"The hilarious thing is that you idiots are defending mr. Corporotocracy himself, Barack Obama, the Wall Street House Negro. I LOVE IT how you tools are scared of Palin and Rand [Paul not Ayn]...love it! No amount of publicity you give to this will change   anything.

i get the impression that people like you, for a variety of reasons, just decided to go along with the JEW World Order... **When we take over, Gentile tools will get it the worst mark my words...dont think im just talking crap behind a computer, we are almost ready."** *And all their intellectual and media tools will be shoved inside forced-labour camps where they will do some honorable work for once in their life. I love it, you are losing, you are scared and i love it!See you in the labour-camps!* **Dont worry ms.Burton i will personally use a few good connections and make you chief-editor of the newspaper of your particular   camp   ;)**

PS – Say hello to WHINEstein for me [referring to Mikey Weinstein, founder of Military Religious Freedom Foundation]

You are probably noticing the use of some of the very same terms by these people. It is common for them to go off talking points. Clearly, some understand the terminology more than others.

Here is one last example. I understand how disturbing it is, but also feel that it is important to share their own vitriol as it is communicated to me. As painful as these are to revisit due to the depth of absolute misinformation that clearly comes straight from the mouths of those like Glenn Beck and his FOX & Friends hate/paranoia channel, it is worth sharing with you. This one will leave you no doubt of the loyalty to Palin, Bachmann and all those conservative "feminists" just like them...

Winter 2010

Hello Ms. Burton,

I heard most of the interview last night on WZTK on Allan Handelman's program. You should thank him for getting your name out (I had never heard of you) and also for screening his callers so that you would not get anyone like me on the air that wanted to suggest that you seemed incredibly jealous of Sarah Palin. (The screener hung up on me when I said that.)

I also wanted to challenge you on your premise that Sarah Palin's agenda is a religious one. Although she is obviously a Christian, I have never heard her try in any way to force her religious views on me or anyone else and I am agnostic. I wanted to ask you if Christian values were a bad trait for a person to have. If you deleted Christianity from America, what would fill the void, as something else surely would - Islam? The tactic you employed against her, Jim Dement, Michell Bachman and the Tea Party in general was pure Alinsky. [somebody's been watching Glenn Beck].

Just as the Tea Party was painted as being racist you try to paint us as religious extremisists when in fact the opposite is the truth. The Tea Party movement provided the only fire and excitement in the last election and the platform is one of smaller government, individual liberty and love of American heritage.

There is a concerted effort to leave issues like abortion out of the discussion, it is simply not relevant to the problems our country faces today. It is always the left that wants to imply that the Tea Party is a bunch of racist religious nuts, when they know darn well that isn't true, in an attempt to marginalize the huge threat the Tea Party represents.

In all your lathered hatred of Sarah Palin yesterday, I was searching for the cause or a reasoned justification but instead I only heard juvenile jealous whining about her attractiveness and zero acknowlegement of her abilities. But I undertsand the reason for your hatred and that is **the huge threat she presents** *that is the reason you and the liberal left despise Sarah Palin, she scares the heck out of you.*

I find the vicious attacks on conservative women by feminists to be rather fascinating, although pathetic. Sarah Plain has a loving relationship with a handsome husband, beautiful children, a career and she happens to be beautiful. She is an awesome example of a modern American woman that I admire. But you can't find ANYTHING good about her.

Christians cause all the problems in America and the Muslims might cut your head off if you make them mad, very brave of you. So yes, you should be terribly afraid of women like Sarah Palin, and me, because we are everywhere in America now.

Look at pictures of the Tea Party rallies, at least half of the people there are women. We are smart, patriotic, and fulfilled with our lives. We know the promise of America and believe in the vision of our Founding Fathers and the promise of individual liberty that America's Constitution guarantees us - and we will fight to defend that way of life every day.

We recognize that liberalism and feminism is really just glossed over socialism and that we are battling against Marxists that don't know how to function or that can't be successful in a Capitalist world. But My Dear, Capitalism and America is responsable for the highest standard of living and the most individual liberty that has ever been present in the history of the world. History also shows that Communism only leads to death,

239

poverty and misery - so why do you want that for America? I know why - you hope you will be one of the few at the top doling out the misery to the idiot masses. Try reading Atlas Shrugged, it is a blue print for how socialism destroys everything. Although everyone hears about the protagonist John Galt, I admire and relate to Dagney's character just as much.

I understand you are depressed and that you and the feminists have to focus on something or someone to vent your frustration on (Sarah Palin) when you see your long held opinions and livelyhoods slipping away at the hands of, OMG - other women! But you need to have a, exscuse the pun, a "come to Jesus moment", figuratively only - of course.

Nobody believes your rants and you sound hollow and insecure on the air and sadly intimidated by Christians and attractive women. Feminisim is going the way of the dial telephone. Get with it, be a truly modern American woman. You just might find it to be a very satifying and invigorating experiance.

I truly appreciate you allowing me this opportunity to express my opinion - and if I didn't care I wouldn't have taken the time to write!

Sincerely,
C. Hughes

I know she will be none too happy to see her letter here, but one has to be able to stand behind their words – which most of them don't. Usually this garbage comes from those who hide behind the name "Anonymous."

But what keeps me going are the emails that come from those who tell me they are learning from me and support my efforts like this one:

"Voices like yours are the lights in the wilderness that are needed. Your mission is not just for you, but for those counting on you."

Fortunately, I get far more of these kind and encouraging emails than I do the hate and ugly threats. It heartens me to hear from people that I am providing information that they have just not heard before and they are listening.

24 Infotainment

"...some on the left, that lamestream media...I want to help clean up the state that is so sorry today of journalism. And I have a communications degree."
~ *Sarah Palin with Sean Hannity Fox News*

Advertising dollars drive what these networks report and almost (as if by accident) they cover stories that actually resemble news on rare occasions. For all of the Right's bellowing for years about the "liberal media" *(just typing that I hear Rush Limbaugh's voice in my head!)*, or the newly coined Palin label, the "lamestream" media, it is truly hard to tell them apart as far as I am concerned. Each side has its own outlet to feed whatever version of reality is most comfortable for them. Left and Right.

The hate mail that I just shared in the last chapter, "Time & Triggers" is inarguably driven by the bombastic information that is broadcast to their viewers on channels like FOX, CBN, GodTV and Daystar. Argue it they will, but words do have tremendous power and influence and these people know it from a marketing perspective.

Few voices pierce through this infotainment industry, and to find those requires effort. You really have to look. They are generally on obscure stations, have minimalist sets and present facts, which we all know are boring and not sexy at all so their audiences are small and their funding almost non-existent.

But the assertion continues that it is the Left that has supernatural powers and controls the media, when the truth is that much of the media in America is owned by conservatives, and many of these are hard-line conservatives. Out of the AM radio stations in America there are over 2,000 conservative radio stations that carry conservative talk shows compared to a paltry 60 or so that air progressive talk radio.

Let's look a little closer at NewsCorp, owners of "FOX News." First, the majority shareholder and owner is Rupert Murdoch, an Australian that sought and received American citizenship in 1985 because of our pesky FCC laws that require that you must be an American citizen to own television stations in the U.S. He also owns many other papers, television stations, movie studios, etc. some of which are: The Wall Street Journal, The New York Post, Daily STAR, (British) Sun, Sky Networks, Metromedia, Fox Searchlight, National Geographic Channel, MCI Communications, DirecTV, Showtime, The Weekly Standard, 20th Century Fox, and a slew of magazines including Vogue, Parents, GQ. On the internet he owns BeliefNet.com, MySpace, Hulu, and then, just for kicks. he owns a couple of publishing companies: HarperCollins and none other than Zondervan which is a Christian publishing company. 37

He is a media magnate that dominates what is broadcast in the print and visual media in America. This isn't bad considering he is an immigrant, that word that Fox News has declared an enemy to our country. Rupe is estimated to be worth a measly $30 billion or more.

Then we have one of the other non-Americans who claims he is second only to Murdoch in his investment in NewsCorp. He is an Islamic extremist named Prince Al-Waleed bin Talal of Saudi Arabia, nephew to the Saudi King, and an "entrepreneur and international investor." With a net worth of "only" $20 billion he still has considerable influences in the United States including ownership (either full or partial) of CitiCorp, CitiBank, Coca-Cola, London's Savoy Hotel, Fairmont Hotels, The Plaza and Four Seasons Hotels, Euro Disney, and investments in AOL. Apple Inc, and Motorola. Of course like Murdoch, this is nowhere near a complete list of their holdings and investments.

John Stewart made the following observations on his comedy show, "The Daily Show:"38

243

Stewart pointed out that Prince Alwaleed can be tied to the Saudi royal family, which finances the construction of Wahabbist mosques, and which has links to the Carlyle Group. The Carlyle Group has, in turn, been tied to Osama bin Laden. And Stewart also pointed out that former New York Mayor Rudy Giuliani rejected a $10-million gift from Prince Alwaleed after the 9/11 attacks, because the Saudi prince had said that US foreign policy contributed to the terrorist attack.

"I think that, really, when you look at this card and you do highlight it in yellow, the only thing you can come up with is: Is Fox News a terrorist command center?" Stewart asked.

Stewart was making a sarcastic point about the logic of those who watch Fox. That they are fed non-news 24/7. They spout hyperbolic vitriol and claim to fear a takeover of America by Islamic extremists who are going to impose Shariah Law, an extremely oppressive form of extreme Islamic law, especially toward women. Yet, they have no fear, no concerns (not even a question or two) about the fact that one of the biggest investors in FOX is not only a Muslim, but a Wahabbist. The Wahabbist are viewed as the Muslim ultra-conservative fundamentalists who hold outdated authoritarian beliefs, much like our own Christian extremists. But, nope. They don't seem to see any conflict in that whatsoever.

That Imam, Faisal Abdul Raif, who wanted to build the Muslim Community Center named Park 51 in New York, blocks away from the site of 9/11 Ground Zero? You remember that whole hoo-ha. Mostly due to FOX News saturation coverage, the story was bought hook, line and sinker that Raif was surely trying to takeover America with his project and turn us all into MusliMs. without any evidence of a direct connection anywhere! They had Raif tied to Hamas for Christ's sake!

This is infotainment. And it is frightening the level of indoctrination and brainwashing that is disseminated across all the airwaves on the Right and the Left that people lap up without questioning. It is dangerous and powerful. We have seen in the past two years how money was able to invent a new political movement that initially called itself the Tea Party. The powers behind the movement were able to make a minority of Americans believe that they were the majority, and then rally them to go forth and work hard to destroy programs that, often, these people actually benefited from.

For example, to bolster this sense of empowerment to a minority Movement, the always-castigated "liberal lamestream media," mouthpiece (a.k.a CNN) even went beyond the call of duty on the evening of President Obama's State of the Union address to Congress by, unbelievably, giving airtime to two rebuttals.

What is the standard procedure here? Obama is a Democrat, so that means that the Republicans got to pick who they thought best would represent them on camera to rebut whatever the President had to say. They chose a young Congressman from Wisconsin, Paul Ryan who requires that his interns in Congress to read Ayn Rand's *Atlas Shrugged* when they come to work for him at the capitol. This is the conservative golden boy who wants to force a voucher system for Medicare and privatize social security among other things. Ryan gave a dismal, fear-soaked, the sky-is-falling-and-we're-all-doomed, *bummer* of a five minute commentary. He, however, took it one step farther, and laid all the ills of the world not just at the feet of the liberals, but Obama himself. In fact, to hear Ryan tell it Obama was so crafty he was secretly pulling the strings and making executive decisions during George Bush, Jr.'s second term. (Who knew?)

But on this occasion, for the first time ever, CNN decided to give equal airtime to the declared Tea Party representative. This was completely unorthodox. First, all Tea Party candidates in office have the Republican 'R' behind their names and so are not differentiated as separate. Second, there have been legitimate members in

Congress over the years that represent other Parties (i.e. Libertarian, Independent, Green Party, etc.) and never have these other Parties been given airtime.

Nevertheless, in a pathetic attempt to prostitute themselves for ratings, CNN allowed Michelle Bachman, who is viewed as the "batshit-crazy" dark haired twin of Palin, to give the rebuttal. And because Bachmann was really speaking into the camera for the Tea Party live streaming internet feed, she looked off to the right of the CNN camera for the entire five-minute diatribe.

It was a transparent attempt to make themselves *part* of the news, rather than report it *(which no one does anymore anyway – well, except for BBC and a handful of others)*. For God's sake! Even the Tea Party infotainment channel Fox, gave her rebuttal a pass! It really is a sporting event, this political game.

So did I miss something here? Did the owners of Fox NewsCorp – Rupert Murdoch, and the Prince buy CNN now when I wasn't looking?

Even in cases where the news doesn't have a specifically conservative slant, the days of Americans being the leaders of news broadcasting are long gone; the closest thing that exists to mainstream progressive "hard news" reporting are international broadcasters such as the BBC, Deutsche Welle, and the French newspaper Le Monde.

Very recently, the skew of American media (and the failure of the American media in catering to infotainment rather than information) became especially apparent. During the rebellions in Egypt and Tunisia, most sources agreed the best and most consistent coverage was from the BBC World Service and from Al-Jazeerah—a Qatari-owned broadcaster largely staffed by former BBC World Service broadcasters for its English-language service.

Most Americans never saw this; if they did, they almost uniformly streamed it over the Internet (either via Al-Jazeerah's own pages or via the official YouTube channel). Al-Jazeerah has found it nearly impossible to be carried on most US cable systems or digital satellite networks, in part because those media outlets are terrified of a mass boycott by Dominionists over "Muslim TV stations;" the only major cable company that carries Al–Jazeerah's English language service is in Washington, D.C., where it is ironically used as a major news source on the happenings in the Middle East by politicians.

Sadly, the days of Robert Murrow and Walter Cronkite are now relegated to the annals of American history.

25 A Twisted Debt of Gratitude

"One vote is victory among many when the many have the majority."

We have come down to this. I have laid out the beginnings of this sad discussion, but I am not going to leave you feeling full of despair. Just because they have behaved badly and gotten away with a great deal up until now, does not mean that it will end that way. We need to take back the control and be assertive and firm about it. That doesn't mean that we have to emulate them and get down in the mud. It isn't an all or nothing issue. Most things aren't.

Every Vote Counts!

Only 36.4 percent of voters cast their ballots in 1998, the lowest since 1942. Nearly two out of three of the 115 million eligible American voters did not bother to vote.

Between 1972 and 2000 the national voting turn-out for the 18-24 year age group declined by 10 percent.

In 1998 less than 20 percent of 18-24 year-olds chose to vote. That is one in five.

In 2000 only 42 percent of 18-24 year-olds bothered to vote. That same year only 75 percent of those older than 25 voted.

When you do not vote, by default you cast your vote against the person or proposal you would prefer. When you do not vote, that vote is one less the opposition has to overcome, thus your "no vote" is a vote for them. The inconveniences of voting is just one small price to pay for the liberty we enjoy. Get up, Get out and vote! – Posted under "voter Trivia"

When Democrats Vote – Democrats Win

Why is this? It is because traditionally there are more registered Democrats in the United states than Republicans, but Republicans vote in much higher numbers as a general rule. Democrats tend to get frustrated and want to pack up their toys and go home. This simply does not work.

This is not about partisan politics at this juncture. I will repeat what I stated earlier. This is not Democrat versus Republican. It is Freedom versus Theocracy/Plutocracy. They don't like to have this direct line drawn, but I am not the one who spent years infesting the Republican Party, taking it over like a cancer and turning it into a religious platform. I am simply pointing out the realities. Religious and Corporate interests are without a doubt more entrenched in the Republican Party than the Democratic Party, which is not to say that the Dems Blue Dogs are remarkably different.

I think of my daughter, a young mother with a very bright future. I think of my four-month old granddaughter who deserves no less than the freedoms and opportunities available to us now... and made better. I think of the next 20 years of my own life and cannot fathom living in an America that is dominated and controlled by those who live in *"Palin's America."*

With the recent uprisings in Tunisia, Sudan, Yemen, and most dramatically in Cairo, Egypt in 2011 it reaffirms that we are damn lucky in this country! Yet oddly enough, it seems to be those that claim to be the proudest Americans of us all who have been known to yell out, *"If you don't like our country just leave!"* to its own citizens.

What I find the most perplexing about those individuals is that I always find them to be the least satisfied with who we are. Their anger, their discontent, their need to control and their pursuit of an autocratic rule are most certainly as un-American as you can get, yet they want *us* to leave. We are the ones who are fighting for equality and tolerance for all whether we ascribe to their beliefs or not.

You have the power of your vote. Do not buy into the rhetoric about how your vote does not matter: It does. I have personally changed the direction of legislation on the Senate Floor by persuading the outcome of one vote. We have had elections in Alaska that were decided by less than 10 votes.

You have the power of your vote. Use it. They depend on your being apathetic and abandoning the notion that it matters. It is the single most important act that you can do to turn this around. The rest of us will continue to fight as full time activists, but we need your help.

Ode to Sarah

If not for her rise, we would not be able to get this message out to so many. Her addiction to media attention and her unquenchable thirst for recognition has given us a perfect star to hang this message on. Now Rick and Michele are bringing up the rear and adding even more attention to this theocratic infestation.

Most of it is not new; ***it has just been hiding in plain sight.***

26 Recommended Web Sites for digging deeper

www.talk2action.com
www.yuricareport.com
www.seekgod.ca
www.politicusUSA.com
www.darkchristianity.com
www.religiondispatches.com
www.darkchristianity.com
www.au.org
www.liarsforjesus.com
www.texasfreedom.com
www.theocracywatch.org
www.discernmentministries.com
www.nolongerquivering.com

27 Recommended Books

With God on Our Side ~ *by Mikey Weinstein*
Spiritual Warfare ~ *by Sarah Dimond*
American Fascists ~ *by Chris Hedges*
Kingdom Coming ~ *by Michelle Goldberg*
The Family & C Street ~ *by Jeff Sharlet*
Crazy for God ~ *by Frank Schaeffer*
It Can Happen Here ~ *by George E. Lowe*
Onward Christian Athletes ~ by Tom Krattenmaker

---

[1] http://charismamag.com/index.php/features/2009/january/20101-the-faith-of-sarah-palin

[2] ibid.

[3] ibid.

[4] http://theresponseusa.com/faq.php.

[5] Andrew Brown, *The Guardian* "Bush, Gog and Magog", 10 August 2009 (http://www.guardian.co.uk/commentisfree/andrewbrown/2009/aug/10/religion-george-bush) via (in French) "George W. Bush et le Code Ezéchiel" (George W. Bush and the Ezekiel Code), *Allez Savoir*, September 2007 available in full online (http://www2.unil.ch/unicom/allez_savoir/as39/pages/pdf/4_Gog_Magog.pdf).

[6] Proudly advertised by Faith and Action, a dominionist lobbying group in Washington (http://www.faithandaction.org/web/2011/07/29/room-219-a-call-to-prayer/); per the website, Randy J. Forbes (R-VA) was the original ringleader, and this has since expanded to a nationwide "prayer network" (http://findroom219.com/aboutus.php); associated congressmen are listed (http://findroom219.com/admemcon.php) and there is an active attempt to set similar "prayer rooms" up in General Assemblies across the US.

[7] Jane Porter, "You Cannot be a Christian and Vote for Obama," http://www.wnd.com/?pageId=79276

[8] Lance Wallnau, "The Seven Mountain Mandate" video seminar series, copyright date unknown. Video seminar series is available at Morningstar Ministries (http://www.morningstarministries.org/Store/Products/1000048500/MorningStar_Store/Specials_and_New/S

pecials/Christmas_Specials/7_Mountain_Mandate.aspx)
; the particular segment is available freely on Youtube
(http://www.youtube.com/watch?v=qQbGnJd9poc&feat
ure=player_embedded) and has been transcribed at the
pro-NAR "Lions of Christ" website
(http://lionsofchrist.blogspot.com/2009/01/7-
mountain-mandate-by-dr-lance-wallnau.html).

9 Bruce Wilson, email interview with Buzzflash
online news magazine
(http://blog.buzzflash.com/articles/interviews/126).

10 Extensively documented by Bruce Wilson, most
notably with "Palin In My Prayer Groups, Says
Witchcraft-Fighting 'Spiritual Warfare' Leader", Talk to
Action, 8 October 2008. The conference in Everett, WA
where Glazier was quoted was held 13 July 2008 and
video of Glazier's speech is available on Youtube
(http://www.youtube.com/watch?v=H5kLreAmgGE&fea
ture=player_embedded).

11 Interview with Loren Cunningham by Os
Hillman and Kelle Hughes, Atlanta, GA, 19 November
2007. Transcribed at "Reclaim Seven Mountains", a pro-
NAR website
(http://www.reclaim7mountains.com/apps/articles/defa
ult.asp?articleid=40087&columnid=4347).

12 *Ibid.*

13 Altermeyer's "The Authoritarians" is available
from his website at
http://home.cc.umanitoba.ca/~altemey/ in PDF format
for free; ebook and paper-book versions are available via
Lulu.com. He has since written a followup, "Comment
On The Tea Party" (available at the same site and also for
free) that identifies the "Tea Party" movement as it exists
as a textbook authoritarian movement.

14 Kyle Mantyla, Right Wing Watch, "Bachmann Intends to Have David Barton Teach Classes on Constitution and Christian History to Members of Congress", December 2010 (http://www.rightwingwatch.org/content/bachmann-intends-have-david-barton-teach-classes-constitution-and-christian-history-members-) via David Brody, *The 700 Club*, 9 December 2010 (The Brody Files, "Gingrich, Bachmann Speak to Brody File About New GOP Congress", http://blogs.cbn.com/thebrodyfile/archive/2010/12/09/gingrich-bachmann-speak-to-brody-file-about-new-gop-congress.aspx which contains 700 Club segment)

15 Quote is actually used on David Barton's official Facebook page (http://www.facebook.com/pages/David-Barton/107999342561866?sk=info) and the linked Wikipedia article; original quote is from Kayla Webley, *Time Magazine*, "Perusing The Glenn Beck University Curriculum Guide", 7 July 2010 (http://newsfeed.time.com/2010/07/07/glenn-beck-university/). This in turn is a paraphrase of an interview of David Barton by Glenn Beck on 29 April 2010 (http://www.glennbeck.com/content/articles/article/196/39831/) wherein Beck claims Barton has the second largest collection of Revolutionary War-era documents, next to the Library of Congress.

16 James C. McKinley Jr, *New York Times*, "Texas Conservatives Win Curriculum Change", 12 March 2010; still available on NYT website (http://www.nytimes.com/2010/03/13/education/13texas.html). Also *ibid.* "Texas Conservatives Seek Deeper Stamp On Texts", 10 March 2010 (http://www.nytimes.com/2010/03/11/us/politics/11texas.html). Also Sam Tanenhaus, *ibid.*, "In Texas Curriculum Fight, Identity Politics Leans Right", 20 March 2010

(http://www.nytimes.com/2010/03/21/weekinreview/21 tanenhaus.html).

    [17] A great deal of info on this is "conspiracy theory" noise, but there IS some verifiable information regarding continuity of government plans from non-conspiracy-theory sites including "dress rehearsals" for instituting COG plans before the 11 September terror attacks; the fact that these COG exercises had taken place and and COG procedures in the event of a national emergency had in fact been enacted as a result of the 11 September attacks were not revealed to Congress or the public until early 2002 and were a separate development from established COG plans developed in the "civil defense" era. Documentaton from reliable sources includes *The Washington Post,* Barton Gellman and Susan Schmidt, "Shadow Government Is at Work in Secret; After Attacks, Bush Ordered 100 Officials to Bunkers Away From Capital to Ensure Federal Survival", 1 March 2002; *CBS News*, Francie Grace, "The Shadow Government", 11 February 2009 (http://www.cbsnews.com/stories/2002/03/02/attack/main502695.shtml); and *The Atlantic*, James Mann, "The Armageddon Plan", March 2004 (republished with permission by Common Dreams, http://www.commondreams.org/views04/0318-14.htm).

In addition, a large portion of the COG functions for the Department of Homeland Security were classified and incorporated under Executive Order in the National Security Presidential Directive 51 passed 9 May 2007 (http://georgewbush-whitehouse.archives.gov/news/releases/2007/05/20070509-12.html). This, too, was done outside of "civil defense" era COG arrangements (particularly the National Emergencies Act of 1976, an Act of Congress explicitly meant to prevent an acting president from declaring a perpetual national emergency). Portions of the document were at a sufficiently high secrecy level that Congressman Peter DeFazio (D-OR), at the time a ranking member of the Homeland Security Committee, was denied access to the classified annexes of NSPD 51 (reported in *The Oregonian,* Jeff Kosseff, "DeFazio Asks, But He's Denied Access", 21 July 2007; reprinted with permission by Common Dreams, http://www.commondreams.org/archive/2007/07/21/2 678). One of the first descriptions of the implications of NSPD 51 as being a potential tool for a coup-de-etat (outside of known conspiracy-theory websites) is *The Progressive*, Matthew Rothschild, "Bush Anoints Himself as the Insurer of Constitutional Government in Emergency", 18 May 2007 (http://progressive.org/mag_wx051807).

[18] full analysis of the reasons for the downfall of the USSR could fill a library in and of itself, but it is generally recognised by most historians that the reasons for the downfall of the USSR were complex and can be linked to inner collapse. Among other things, there is very good documentation (especially with the states of Latvia, Lithuania, and Estonia which were incorporated into the USSR in the early 40s) that anti-Russian sentiment had a great deal to do with why they were the first states to break away (the incorporation was not widely recognised in the West, and to this day Russo-Latvians are not generally eligible for full citizenship unless they give up any claims to Russian nationality) and there were major tensions between Russia, the Caucasus states of Georgia and Armenia, and the Moslem-majority states that were in part a result of forced Russification of these ethnic groups (http://www.globalsecurity.org/military/world/war/russia1.htm and http://www.historyorb.com/russia/ethnic_problems.sht ml have some very good discussion of the complexity of the downfall of the Soviet Union).

Frances FitzGerald's *Way Out There In The Blue* also details how military personnel behind the SDI or "Star Wars" effort knew that the USSR was close to economic collapse and that in particular military spending by the USSR had been flat throughout the 80s.. Interestingly, she also notes in the same book that the *perestroika* reforms in the late 80s may have actually been what pushed the USSR to the brink of collapse (http://www.j-bradford-delong.net/politics/fitzgerald.html).

It is of particular note that--contrary to the claims of some--not all of the states of the former USSR ended up as democracies. One state in particular, Turkmenistan, ended up as a police state/cult-state surrounding the personality cult around Saparmurat Niyazov that rivaled the *Juche* cult-state instituted by the Kim dynasty in North Korea (a good "mainstream" news source detailing the Niyazov regime is *CBS News*, Mary-Jayne McKay, "Turkmenbashi Everywhere", 11 February 2009 (http://www.cbsnews.com/stories/2003/12/31/60minut es/main590913.shtml)); another ex-USSR state, Belarus, has consistently been labeled the last "Warsaw Pact style state" in Europe and has been under dictatorship rule since the time it split from the USSR (a good article on Belarus is *The Guardian*, "Europe's last dictatorship", 2 March 2006 (http://www.guardian.co.uk/g2/story/0,,1721135,00.htm l) and reliable international news sources indicate the situation has actually worsened since that report).Need footnote

[19] Bill Press, *Spin This!: All the Ways We Don't Tell the Truth*, pg. 80 (Simon and Schuster, 2001) as paraphrased in "The Ronald Reagan Myth", *The Progressive Review* (Simon and Schuster, 2001). The book Press is referring to is *Way Out There in the Blue: Reagan, Star Wars and the End of the Cold War*,

Frances FitzGerald (Simon and Schuster, 2000).Need footnote

[20] http://www.rightweb.irc-online.org/profile/Council_for_National_Policy

[21] Liberty Sunday (the rebranding of the Justice Sunday) events is acknowledged by FRC on its own website (http://www.frc.org/get.cfm?c=FRC_SIMULCAST); documentation of FRC being ringleader of "Justice Sunday" events is via a PDF of an FRC newsletter at Sky Angel's website (http://www.skyangel.com/_FileLibrary/File/0610_Liberty_Sunday_Article.pdf?IdS=0012AD-7684D50&); Sky Angel is a dominionist-friendly DSS provider that has telecasted the Justice Sunday and Liberty Sunday events on its "public access" channel (Alex Bird writing as "dogemperor", *Talk to Action*, "Dominionism and racists and Justice Sunday III" 10 April 2006 and *ibid*, *Daily Kos*, "Dominionism's "parallel economy", part 6: Modern dominionist broadcasting", 31 July 2007. Press releases for FRC and its partnership with Sky Angel for telecasts of Justice Sunday events are still available from PR Newswire (http://www.prnewswire.com/news-releases/frc-partners-with-sky-angel-to-broadcast-justice-sunday-ii-54681127.html).

[22] Connections between the FRC and neo-Confederate groups are close enough that the linkages were one reason FRC was recently listed by SPLC as a hate group; more particularly, the purchase of the Knights of the Ku Klux Klan mailinglist by Perkins from David Duke is well documented (Max Blumenthal, *The Nation,* "Justice Sunday Preachers", 26 April 2005 (http://www.thenation.com/article/justice-sunday-preachers) which also details speeches by Tony Perkins to the SPLC-listed Council of Conservative Citizens--the modern day "white citizen's councils").

23 Explicitly quoted in PDF from parentalrights.org (http://www.parentalrights.org/vertical/Sites/%7BC491 08C5-0630-467E-9B9B-B1FA31A72320%7D/uploads/%7B49DFD684-E041-4BA1-AD54-42EE54A0464B%7D.PDF); parentalrights.org is a front-group of Home School Legal Defense Association (both orgs are run by Michael Farris), a dominionist correspondence-schooling "homeschooling" lobbying group promoting corresondence-schooling to the exclusion of secular and inclusive homeschooling and unschooling programs. Parentalrights.org is promoting a "Parental Rights Amendment" that would strip practically all jurisdiction from child welfare agencies in regards to abuse complaints (http://www.parentalrights.org/index.asp?Type=B_BASI C&SEC={D7513A40-0E77-4052-96CE-F357CE36B649}&DE=). The HSLDA linkage becomes important as HSLDA state affiliates have in fact done coaching on how to "buffalo" CPS investigations resulting from religiously motivated child abuse (http://www.nathhan.com/howtosocial.htm) and the org itself has essentially promoted dominionist correspondence-schooling as a method to hide signs of religiously motivated child abuse from mandatory reporters (http://hsislegal.com/?s=CPS).

24 Loren Cunningham, interview with Os Hillman and Kelle Hughes, *ibid*.

25 Brig. Gen. Charles Duke, as quoted by Ann Patton *Academy Spirit*, "Prayer luncheon guest speaker recalls wonder of space", 10 February 2010 (http://www.usafa.af.mil/news/story.asp?id=123190072) . *Academy Spirit* is the official student newspaper of the US Air Force Academy, Colorado Springs.

26 http://godsownparty.com/blog/2010/01/call-it-irony-call-it-kharma-call-it-gods-will/

[27] Quite a lot of documentation on Shoebat exists, including by Chip Berlet (*Talk to Action*, "Walid Shoebat's Apocalyptic Islamophobia", 24 March 2011 (http://www.talk2action.org/story/2011/3/24/63741/57 39)), Chris Rodda (*ibid.*, ""Obsession" Stars Have Lectured at U.S. Military Colleges; U.S. Navy Uses Film", 17 September 2008 (http://www.talk2action.org/story/2008/9/17/15847/70 77) and Richard Bartholomew--by far the most prolific writer on Shoebat (*ibid.*, "Texas Attorney General to Promote Walid Shoebat at "Homeland Security" Conference", 19 July 2008 (http://www.talk2action.org/story/2008/7/19/125738/0 86)).

Investigation as to the authenticity of Shoebat's story (of being an ex-terrorist) include prolific articles by Bartholomew (*Talk to Action*, "Walid Shoebat: The Simon Altaf Connection", 2 July 2008 (http://www.talk2action.org/story/2008/7/2/92119/235 24); *ibid.*, "Walid Shoebat Denounced by Former Co-Author", 26 February 2009 (http://www.talk2action.org/story/2009/2/26/193721/8 87); *ibid.*, "The Continuing Absurdity of Walid Shoebat", 28 September 2008 (http://www.talk2action.org/story/2008/9/28/13035/0 736)) as well as *Jerusalem Post*, Jorg Luyken, "The Palestinian 'Terrorist' Turned Zionist", 30 March 2008 (http://www.jpost.com/Features/Article.aspx?id=96502) . CNN investigations have also turned up serious holes in the story ("'Ex-terrorist' rakes in homeland security bucks", 13 July 2011 (http://articles.cnn.com/2011-07-11/us/terrorism.expert_1_walid-shoebat-israeli-police-homeland-security?_s=PM:US)).
Bruce Wilson has also noted there is a strong possibility that Walid Shoebat is a fraud (*Talk to Action*, "McCain Backer Hagee Showcases 'Islamic Terrorist' Implicated as

Possible Fraud", 1 April 2008
(http://www.talk2action.org/story/2008/4/1/10565/383
08/Dominionism_in_the_military/McCain_Backer_Ha
gee_Showcases_Islamic_Terrorist_Implicated_as_Possi
ble_Fraud).

My associate Alex Bird has also found some potential
evidence of deeper fraud akin at least to the Mike Warnke
fraud of the 80s (Bird writing as "dogemperor", *Talk to
Action*, "The 'Walid Shoebat' Con Game--Exposed!", 1
April 2008)--in particular, there are striking similarities
in appearance of "Shoebat" and his supposed manager,
Kevin Davies) and Davies is known to promote an entire
industry surrounding "convertee Enemy" stories,
including a supposed ex-*Hitlerjugend* who supposedly
became a neopentecostal convertee and the fact that
"Walid Shoebat" is apparently an alias.

Discussion of the "convertee Enemy" being a common
trope in neopentecostal Christianity (one that goes
beyond "convertee Moslems" but which included--
infamously--"ex-Satanists" in the 80s until "Christian
comedian" and self-proclaimed "ex-Satanist" Mike
Warnke was outed as a fraud in *Cornerstone Magazine*)
include *The Washington Post,* Omar Sacirbey, "Skeptics
challenge life stories offered by high-profile Muslim
converts to Christianity", 26 June 2010
(http://www.washingtonpost.com/wp-
dyn/content/article/2010/06/25/AR2010062504435.ht
ml and the article focuses primarily on the "convertee
Moslem" variant of the trope).

[28] David Koch, as quoted by Nathan Diebenow,
Raw Story, "Tea party financier: 'Rank and file' members
are just like me", 12 January 2011
(http://www.rawstory.com/rs/2011/01/12/tea-party-
financier-thinks-rank-file/).

[29] As early as 1998 the combined worth of Koch Industries was estimated at US$35B by the *New York Times* (Leslie Wayne, "Zero Is the Verdict in $2 Billion Koch Family Feud", 20 June 1998 (http://www.nytimes.com/1998/06/20/business/zero-is-the-verdict-in-2-billion-koch-family-feud.html)) and has also been quoted by the same newspaper at this worth as recently as 2011 (*ibid.*, Bob Herbert, "When Democracy Weakens", 11 February 2011 (http://www.nytimes.com/2011/02/12/opinion/12herbert.html)).

[30] Main inheritance estimate from *Wonkette*, "Here's How the Koch Bros. Put 'Raise the Retirement Age' On TV", 22 June 2011 (http://wonkette.com/448131/heres-how-the-koch-bros-put-raise-the-retirement-age-on-tv) and from public records.Need source.

[31] David Koch, *ibid.*

[32] http://en.wikipedia.org/wiki/Cato_Institute

[33] http://www.greenpeace.org/usa/en/campaigns/global-warming-and-energy/polluterwatch/koch-industries/mercatus-center/

[34] http://www.sourcewatch.org/index.php?title=Americans_for_Prosperity

[35] http://www.freedomworks.org/about/board-of-directors/steve-forbes

[36] Mich McConnell, as quoted by *Chicago Tribune*, Michael A. Memoli, "Mitch McConnell's remarks on 2012 draw White House ire", 27 October 2010 and reprinted with permission by the *Los Angeles Times* (http://articles.latimes.com/2010/oct/27/news/la-pn-obama-mcconnell-20101027). The quote was sufficiently

infamous that it ended up as "Bonus Quote Of The Day" on 25 October 2010's *Political Wire* (http://politicalwire.com/archives/2010/10/25/bonus_q uote_of_the_day.html).

37 A list of all known NewsCorp holdings is available on Wikipedia based on compliations from the various corporate news sites of NewsCorp (http://en.wikipedia.org/wiki/List_of_assets_owned_by _News_Corporation); in the particular case of Zondervan, it is now an imprint of HarperCollins which is a NewsCorp holding (http://www.newscorp.com/management/harperc.html).

Not listed here is the British *Sunday Times*, which was forced to shut down over a massive "phone hacking" scandal including unauthorised access to voice mail systems of cellphones of victims of an infamous murder. There may be ongoing implications for NewsCorp's ownership of many media properties in the UK as a result.

38John Stewart, *The Daily Show*. as quoted by *Raw Story,* David Edwards and Daniel Tencer, "Stewart: 'Is Fox News a terrorist command center?'", 20 August 2010 (http://www.rawstory.com/rs/2010/08/20/stewart-fox-terrorist-command-center/). The particular segment is available on Comedy Central's website (http://www.thedailyshow.com/watch/thu-august-19-2010/extremist-makeover---homeland-edition).